GILROY'S OLD CITY HALL

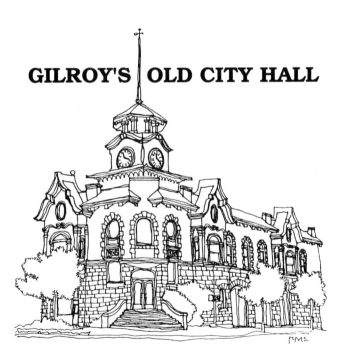

Angela Woollacott and Carroll Pursell with Chuck Myer

GILROY'S OLD CITY HALL

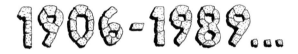

1906-1989...

by Angela Woollacott and Carroll Pursell
with Chuck Myer

Foreword by Kathryn Gualtieri, California State Historic Preservation Officer

Local History Studies Volume 34
California History Center
Cupertino, California

For the people
of Gilroy

Sponsored by the Gilroy Bicentennial Committee and the Gilroy Historical Society.

Edited by Chuck Myer and James C. Williams.
Designed by James C. Williams.
Copyright © by the City of Gilroy, 1991.
All rights reserved, including the right of
reproduction in any form. Published by the
California History Center and Foundation, De Anza College
21250 Stevens Creek Blvd., Cupertino, California 95014.

10 9 8 7 6 5 4 3 2 1

First Edition

Library of Congress Cataloging-in-Publication Data

Woollacott, Angela, 1955–
    Gilroy's Old City Hall, 1906-1989– / by Angela Woollacott and Carroll Pursell with Chuck Myer;
    foreword by Kathryn Gualtieri. – 1st ed.
        p. cm. – (Local History Studies, ISSN 0276-4105; v.34)

Includes index

ISBN 0-935089-15-2: $19.95

1. Old City Hall (Gilroy, CA)   2. Old City Hall Restaurant (Gilroy, CA)   3. Gilroy (CA) – Buildings, structures, etc.

I. Pursell, Carroll, 1932–   II. Myer, Chuck, 1954–   III. Title.   IV. Series.

F869.G48W66 1991   90-25870
979.4'73–dc20   CIP

CONTENTS

FOREWORD

At the beginning of the twentieth century a significant part of our state's population resided in urban centers like San Francisco and Oakland in Northern California, and Los Angeles in the south. These population spores grew because, in the eyes of many, cities could provide better municipal services that improved upon the quality of life for Californians.

By contrast, many small towns throughout the state still offered a rural environment in 1900. Population in these places increased at a very slow pace. Agricultural production, however, surged, largely because of the availability of an abundant labor supply.

Communities like Gilroy in Santa Clara County served the local farmers, who marketed their products to the larger cities. As did other similar sized towns at the turn of the century, Gilroy, with a population of under 2,000 people, experienced a desire for civic and economic development, a desire to "progress" and "improve".

With the building of the new Gilroy City Hall in 1905-06, little did the public-spirited citizens of the times realize that their efforts would be highly appreciated some eight decades later by the current residents of this charming community, as well as by other people from throughout California who value the historical and architectural significance of their landmark public building in the heart of downtown.

As you will read in the pages to come, the history of Gilroy can be said to epitomize the histories of many other California rural supply centers which served the needs of the agricultural communities surrounding them. What sets Gilroy apart is the effort that continues to be made by its citizens to preserve the major symbol of the town's heritage, at a time when so many other towns and cities are destroying, or have already destroyed, their important civic landmarks. Rather than having a replica building, Gilroy citizens believe there is nothing better than having "the real thing." I heartily agree!

The Gilroy City Hall has been recognized over the years by many noted groups and organizations, as well as by the State of California. The California Historical Society and the Conference of California Historical Societies called for its preservation early on. The Native Daughters of the Golden West honored it with a historical plaque some twenty years ago. Of equal importance was the nomination of the building to the National Register of Historic Places by the City Council in 1974, an action which was combined with a strong commitment by the City to assist developers in its restoration and reuse.

Restoration work on the building was a mixed blessing. One can point with pride to the exterior renovation, including the preservation of the fine old town clock. However, misguided efforts by one group of developers in the early 1980s, who removed valuable historic fabric from the significant upstairs courtroom, proved disasterous. This type of project would not be recommended by even a neophyte preservationist today. It was correct of Al Gagliardi, a member of the city's Historical Heritage Committee at the time, to express strong disapproval of the inappropriate work being done. If he had not done so, then perhaps a later developer might not have been willing to put the courtroom back to its pre-"restoration" state.

Not *all* buildings deserve preservation. However, in the case of the Gilroy City Hall, a historic preservationist would urge that this unique focal point be protected and preserved for all time. In the past five years, city officials and local preservationists have struggled to reopen the City Hall, at tremendous odds. By their efforts they hope to return the handsome monument to a useful purpose and rightful place in the city's heritage.

Through the 1984 California Park and Recreational Facilities Bond Act and 1989 emergency funding for earthquake-damaged structures, the State has attempted to assist these local efforts by awarding grants of some $63,000 to begin to save the building.

I lend my full support to the worthy endeavor. The Gilroy City Hall stands as a reminder to all of us of our past. It serves as an outstanding example of a local effort to preserve an important cultural link with Gilroy's historic heritage. Without these local treasures in our midst, what will we have to challenge us to preserve the significant landmarks of future generations?

Kathryn Gualtieri
California State Historic
Preservation Officer

ACKNOWLEDGEMENTS

We wish to thank Mary Prien and Patricia Snar of the Gilroy Historical Museum for their generous help during the research for this book, and Chuck Myer of the City of Gilroy Planning Department for his assistance. Much of the important research material used came from people interviewed, for whose friendly cooperation we also are grateful. All Gilroy citizens, they are: Virginia Cox, Albert Gagliardi, Roberta Hughan, Judge John Klarich, Elizabeth and Philip Lawton, Patricia Baker Loveless, Mary Prien, Frances Howson Vigna, and George White.

Our thanks also go to those individuals and organizations who have seen to the publication of *Gilroy's Old City Hall, 1906-1989,* but particularly to James C. Williams, of the Old City Hall Committee and California History Center Foundation, who worked with Chuck Myer to copy edit and design this work and see it through the publication process.

Angela Woollacott
Carroll Pursell

Supplemental interviews conducted between 1985-1990 also were used in the completion of this document. In addition to those listed above, these interviews were with: Jay Baksa, Ralph Blackburn, Byron and Rhoda Bolfing, Gene Corriden, Steade Craigo, Michael Dorn, Millard Dove, George Espinola, Charles Gilmore, Russ Hendrickson, Sandoe Hanna, Roger and Jeff Hoffman, Doris Kallas, Nancy McCarthy, Marion Mitchell-Wilson, Frank Pattie, Kendall Pine, Cecil Reinsch, Howard Smith, Pat Snar, Susanne Steinmentz, and Fred Wood.

Also, I would like to express my appreciation to the following agencies for their assistance: the California Pioneers of Santa Clara County, Center Stage, the City of Gilroy, *Gilroy Dispatch,* the Gilroy Historical Museum, Gilroy Historical Society, California State Office of Historic Preservation, the *San Jose Mercury News,* and the Old City Hall Restaurant.

Chuck Myer

I. Reflecting Credit Upon Our People: Gilroy's Old City Hall

by Angela Woollacott and Carroll Pursell

PLEASANT VALLEY: A Thriving and Spirited Community

Long before Gilroy established its renown as the "Garlic Capital of the World," and even before it boasted of itself as the "Home of the Prune," it was known as "Pleasant Valley." This valley was part of the Santa Clara Valley, which laid its claim to being the "Garden of the World." The robust pride and appreciation of the advantages of the natural environment which all of these appellations reflect have been integral to the fabric of Gilroy's history since the first non-Hispanic Europeans settled there. Since the early growth of the township in the mid-19th century, Gilroy has been characterized by a self-conscious optimism.

John (Cameron) Gilroy, the Scottish sailor who parted from his ship in Monterey in 1814 to become the first of the new wave of settlers, had the honor of seeing his name bestowed on the town in 1867. Other early settlers included Thomas Doak (1822), Julius Martin (1843), and Henry Miller, who began buying land in the area in 1863. Development

proceeded quickly in the 1850s with the building of an inn, a store, a hotel, a blacksmith's shop, a saddler's shop, a post office, a school, a Methodist Episcopal church and a Catholic chapel. The blossoming of California as a key state of the union after the turbulence of the Gold Rush was reflected in the firm foundation of a community in Gilroy.

The growth of the 1850s and 1860s culminated in 1868 with the incorporation of Gilroy as a town on February 18, 1868. Town officers were elected the next month. In March 1870, the state legislature passed an act incorporating Gilroy as a city, with a full charter and governmental structure; the first set of city officers and councilmembers were elected in May. This new entity, the City of Gilroy, assembled itself with a vision toward expansion and prosperity.

By 1890, according to census data, the population of Gilroy had grown to 1,694. The population had more than doubled by 1930, when it was 3,502. In 1970 Gilroy could boast of a population of 12,665, and by 1990 the City had topped the 30,000 mark. Gilroy's history is that of a thriving and spirited community.

A community instantly and visibly displays itself in its built form. The architecture of a city is an important clue to both its character and its history. In Gilroy, the Old City Hall is the city's most important and distinctive symbol. Built in 1905-06 as a flagship for Gilroy's economic and community development, its unique, even flamboyant style has been an integral part of the character of Gilroy ever since. The story of Gilroy has been played out within and around the building, while the City Hall became known as a landmark throughout California.

George T. Dunlap, Mayor of Gilroy.
The Gilroy Museum

A STONE EDIFICE: Building The City Hall

Over the years, the citizens of Gilroy faced the normal responsibilities for civic improvements. The town, by its fourth decade, looked much like other small, agriculturally-based communities in the state.[1] The beginning of a new century, however, seemed to have nourished a certain discontent in the breasts of some of the "progressive" citizens, a feeling of dissatisfaction with the old and a yearning to get on with the new age. Looking at San Luis Obispo, Hollister, Los Gatos and other communities, the *Gilroy Advocate* complained early in 1904 that "Towns of fewer natural advantages are steadily forging ahead of Gilroy. Some of our valley settlements bid fair in a few years to outdo us in population and enterprise. To make progress," it concluded, "we must get out of our dormant condition and show more public spirit...."[2]

Fortunately, the desire was met by the means. As a contemporary *Souvenir Magazine of Gilroy* noted, almost as a toast to the city's future, Gilroy was a part of "The Undeveloped Empire of Santa Clara Valley. Ever Responsive to the Touch of Capital, Industry and Enterprise."[3] The old Gilroy Board of Trade had become the Promotion Society (and later the present-day Chamber of Commerce), but the larger hopes for "improvement" centered on the city election during the Spring of 1904. What the *Advocate* called "a Ticket Of Progressive Business Men," headed by George T. Dunlap as candidate for Mayor, presented itself to the electorate as the best hope for civic improvement.[4]

A bit of doggerel poetry, published in the local newspaper, entitled "If I Were Mayor of This Beautiful Town," and to be "sung to ragtime," captured the jaunty optimism over future possibilities:

I would put the present City Hall on a frame, if I were Mayor of this beautiful town... [Chorus] If I were Mayor of this beautiful town, If I were Mayor of this beautiful town, Gilroy would be a City of life and renown, if I were Mayor of this beautiful town.[5]

Dunlap had been born in 1862 (he died in 1932) and was in 1904 a prominent member of the business community, being head of the Dunlap Realty and Produce Company ("who are among the largest and most prominent dealers in real estate, livestock, grain and fruit in this section of the State"), as well as a proprietor of the Coyote Cattle Company and president of the South Santa Clara Fruit Drying and Packing Company.[6] He was apparently the type of person the city wanted, because the "Progressive Business Men" won not only the mayor's office, but three City Council seats as well. It was a clear mandate for what that group defined as Progress.[7]

In his inaugural speech, the new Mayor declared a "new era in the history of Gilroy" and sketched a program of improvement which was as diverse as it was ambitious. He mentioned a new city park and other desirable improvements but declared that "nothing is a better index of the enterprise and stability of a community than the general appearance and character of its public buildings. In the case of our city there is certainly nothing of which we have reason to be proud, and much that may be greatly improved with a small outlay. We shall be sadly delinquent as a city if we do not give early and earnest thought to the subject of erecting a new city hall, eligibly located, and of such general character as will at once meet the needs of the public and reflect credit upon our people." Addressing the new City Council directly, he charged them to "let this subject have a prominent place in your consideration at the earliest date practicable."[8]

The earliest date proved to be the Council meeting of August 1, 1904. After an executive session, the Council resolved "to immediately proceed to the erection of a new City Hall," which was somewhat optimistically estimated to cost only $15,000. At the same time, indicating considerable private conversation prior to the meeting, it was resolved to hire the San Jose architectural firm of Wolfe and McKenzie "to prepare plans and specifications for the same."[9]

The bare account recorded in the City Council Minutes was fleshed out for the citizens in the next issue of the *Gilroy Advocate*. "A stone edifice is sugged for the City Hall," it reported, "one of tasteful design, commodious and in every way equal to the wants of the Council, the firemen and the citizens. The exterior would be entirely of stone, quarried from the Gilroy Hills, and the interior constructed of local material as far as possible. This handsome building," it continued, "will front on Monterey street, the high basement for the firemen's service to cover a hall of meeting and the apparatus of the department. The second story, approached by a broad flight of stone steps, to embrace an assembly room with a seating capacity of three hundred." In additions, "other rooms are contemplated for the use of the Board of Trade, and for a permanent show of local products for the view of visitors. The clock tower and flag staff will give finish to the building. A space of fifty feet or more on the east side will be used for a court yard with grass plot and fountain. The era of progress," it concluded, "dawns upon the town under Mayor Dunlap's administration."[10]

That same week it was revealed that Santa Clara

San Jose Post Office with
Saint Joseph's Church
and electric light tower
in the background,
c.1900.
*The California History
Center*

3506 The Post Office, St. Joseph's Church, and Electric Tower, 250 feet high, San Jose, California

County was planning to build "a branch county jail" in the city, to be built of brick at a cost of $5,000. The *Advocate* noted that "the county seat (in San Jose) is thirty miles away and the need for a jail at this end of the county has often been unpleasantly pressed upon the officers."[11] Mayor Dunlap had suggested in his inaugural address that the county might be induced to make this jail a part of the new City Hall. When the Supervisors did indeed vote funds for the jail in late september, it appeared that a significant part of the new building's funding would thus be obtained from the County.[12]

The *Advocate* rejoiced that the City Council was "moving in the right direction to give Gilroy a more attractive appearance to the many who are coming to the State to seek homes and places of investment."[13] During the first week of September, under the headline "City Hall and Jail Building," is noted that:

A colored sketch of the stone building which is designed to cover a new town hall, fire department and jail for this city is on exhibition in Cobb & Wood's show window. This attractive picture with the drafted plan of the buildings command much attention. Wolfe & McKenzie of San Jose are architects and draftsmen. The building will be of brownstone, two stories high, with clock tower. Its appearance bears resemblance to the San Jose post office building. The site for its erection is most centrally located. It will occupy the frontage of the north side of Sixth street, extending from Monterey street to Railroad Avenue. The floor plans show the first story a basement arranged for the service of the firemen. A wide stone stairway leads to the upper floor where the Council chamber, clerk's office and assembly hall. There will be desks in the council chambers for the gas and water superintendents and for the press reporters. The Firemen will have a spacious assembly hall on the ground floor, a justice court and offices are provided. The jail connected on the east side will contain six cells and a bathroom....

A range of public buildings so unique in design and combination at a location open to the view of all, will prove a splendid advertisement to the town. A building of this class with its four-sided clock tower

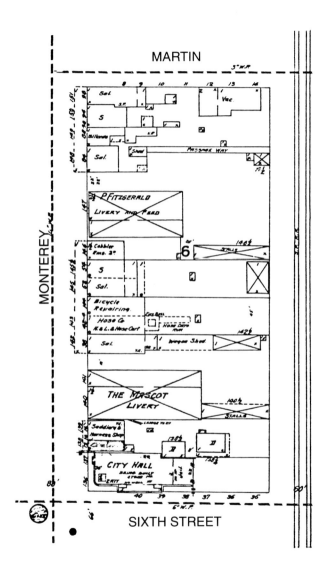

City Hall site, on the corner of Sixth Street and Monterey This 1906 Sanborn Fire Insurance map also shows the saddlery and harness shop next door, which eventually became Paul's Trading Post. Further north on Monterey are livery stables, a cobbler's shop, billiards hall, and various other businesses.
The Gilroy Museum

would be out of place wedged in between stables in connection with a range of old style '49 tenements. On the corner selected, these handsome buildings will command admiration at sight--here is nothing to obstruct the view.

Sixth Street is the central and only road crossing Monterey street, our main business avenue. Not far hence, as ranches east are subdivided and sold for homes, Sixth Street will be the grand highway or boulevard from the Glen Ranch to Old Gilroy. The making of roads through the large holdings east will add to their value. Citizens should look ahead and build for the future, and merchants and tradesmen have an eye to all improvements promotive of increased settlement. The majority favor this policy and conclude that the city council and the supervisors are wise in giving this eligible corner lot their favorable consideration for the public buildings contemplated.[14]

At the next Council meeting, on September 6th, the decision was made to go ahead and purchase the Hotaling property at the corner of Sixth and Monterey for the new City Hall, so long as it could be purchased for no more than $3,500. The *Advocate* rejoiced that "the vigor of life is in the movements of the present Council," noted that they "wisely concluded with the business men and the heaviest taxpayers of the city that this is the most central and appropriate site," and concluded "Go ahead, gentlemen. The progressive people are with you."[15] A special meeting of the Council had to be called late in September to discuss the apparently clouded title of the property, but it decided that the Mayor was capable of sorting the matter out. On October 3rd, the Mayor announced that the "purchase had been consummated and that the deeds were in preparation."[16]

During these same months the Mayor and Council were also in frequent contact with the architect, Frank D. Wolfe, senior partner of the San Jose firm of Wolfe and McKenzie. Wolfe had been born in Ohio during the Civil War and had been practicing in San Jose since before 1900.[17] The Council repeatedly approved the plans and specifications that Wolfe presented but always reserved the right to make modifications as they suggested themselves.[18]

On October 27th, the Council voted to accept bids for the foundation work on the new building, but when they were opened on November 7th, they ranged from $1,124 to $2,176. It was decided to reject them all. Wolfe was in attendance and stated that "the foundation was designed for the same kind of soil as the I.O.O.F. Home, but if the ground would permit he could reduce the size of the foundation, and it would still be adequate. He said he could drill the ground and make plans accordingly." He was instructed to "prepare plans for a smaller foundation if practical, specifying Golden Gate or

Standard Cement."[19]

The new bids for the foundation, when opened on November 12th, ranged from $500 to $723. The low bid of M.E. Kilcourse was accepted, and two days later the Council entered into an agreement with him for the construction. In the absence of the architect, two Council members volunteered to supervise the work. On December 20th the job was declared "completed" and "well done," and Kilcourse was paid off.[20]

Meanwhile it was decided also to move ahead with the contract for the stone work, because "it would take some time to quarry the stone." When bids were opened on November 26th, there were only two: one by J.W. Williams for $2,400 and one from the Granite Rock Co. for $1,475. The latter was accepted.[21] Early in January, 1905, negotiations apparently hit some sort of snag, for the company requested that the Council hold off on the signing of the contract until the latter were prepared to actually authorize the start of construction. The Council agreed.[22] By April, however, the *Gilroy Gazette* was noting that "Many inquiries have been made as to why things are at a standstill with the new City Hall."[23] Its explanation seemed thin:

It may be good for the foundation to have the opportunity to settle well but as a general thing there is a desire to see more than the foundation on the

ground. Work it is said will be resumed on the structure as soon as the stone can be hauled to town from the quarry west of town and that is governed entirely by the quantity of water in the stream.

The cause of the City's delay is not explicit in the Council minutes, but no doubt was the result of escalating costs. The original estimate of $15,000 for the entire job had been overly optimistic. Additionally, as late as the beginning of May the Santa Clara Board of Supervisors had not yet approved of the site and plans for the proposed branch jail. As the *Gilroy Gazette* noted, "until that is done the building will really remain at a stand-still." When they finally appeared on the site, it was reported that "none of the Supervisors expressed any opinion on the subject, yet the comments casually made and the questions asked would point to the conclusion that they were satisfied with the plans and the proposed location of the building."[24] Apparently the Supervisors backed off from their commitment, and the County funds were not forthcoming. In the face of this problem, and because funds were needed for a series of other improvements as well, the City decided to put a bond issue to a vote of the citizens.[25]

In June the City Engineer, Edgar A. Holloway, reported the monies needed for each of the contemplated improvements: $5,000 additional for the City Hall, $10,000 for the water works, $11,000 for a municipal electric plant, and $22,830 for a sewer system. The Council accepted these figures and passed the necessary ordinances to put the matter before the voters. A resolution from the Gilroy Ladies Auxiliary of the Promotion Society "encouraged" the Council to persist, and the voters sent the same message. In August, 423 voters took to the polls and passed the bond issue for all four improvements by substantial margins.[26]

With the money provided for, the Council turned back to the plans and asked Wolfe to come up with alternative sketches, ones which would reduce the cost of the entire project. The Council itself decided "that the large room for the county prisoners should not be fitted with cells at the present time, also that the yard at the rear of the building intended for the prisoners, and which was an unsightly one story lean-to should be left off." By the end of the month, Wolfe had his modifications on paper:

The first one submitted reduced the height of the building: left the bell tower open with the clock up in the cupola above the bell. General objection was made to the changes in this that the design was not pleasing and the clock would be hard to get at.

The second sketch put the clock down over the main entrance but provided for only one dial face: the tower lower and the roof flatter.

The third sketch gave the building a flat roof with

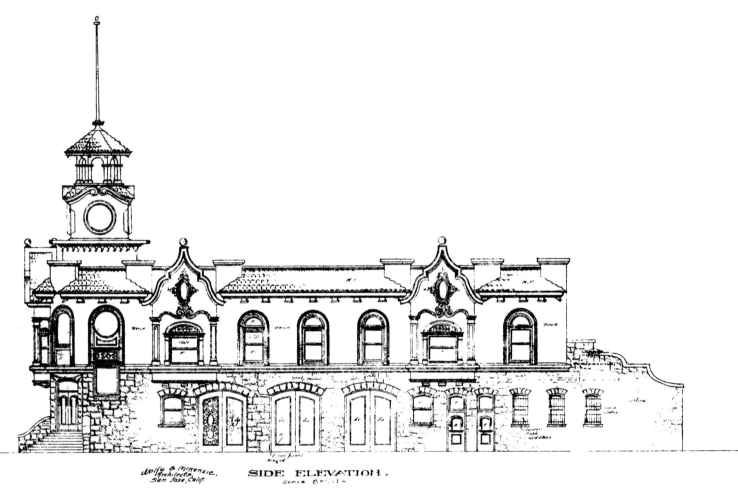

Wolfe & McKenzie,
Architects,
San Jose, Calif.

SIDE ELEVATION.
Scale 8ft = 1 in.

From the original plans.
The Gilroy Museum

plain front, no ornamentation, with clock in lower part of the tower...

After a thorough examination and discussion the consensus of opinion was unanimously against any modification of the plans as originally prepared. The general feeling was to the effect that the public would not favor any alterations of the design which would mar in any way the beauty of the structure even though a slight saving in the cost would result. It will be many years before another City Hall is built and it should be constructed with consideration to its sightly exterior as well as interior usefulness....

Grey stone is to be the material of which the lower story will be built. The second story to be of compressed white brick and above that terra cotta coping with a red tile roof. This combination of colors will make a very attractive and artistic building.[27]

The slightly modified plans were adopted on September 11, 1905, and bids were called for the building's construction. Once again the Granite Rock Company of Watsonville was low bidder, at $19,890.[28] George Seay, who had been born in Kentucky but come to Gilroy in 1888, was made foreman of the works, and stone for the building was quarried from the Indian Camp area of Henry Miller's nearby Glen Ranch.[29]

On October 27th the *Gilroy Gazette* happily reported that:

Indian Camp Quarry on the Glen Ranch.
The Gilroy Museum

There is something doing on the lot at the corner of Monterey and Sixth Streets.

A few men are at work cutting stone and a number of men are standing by watching them. It therefore looks as though the work on the City Hall has actually commenced. A large quantity of mortar has been mixed and stone and brick hauled on the ground and Wednesday morning a start was made in laying the stone of which the first story is to be built. The building was commenced at the northwest corner of the foundation, that is the corner adjoining Winkler's harness shop and the evidences are that the building will go up very rapidly. For every man who is at work there are about four onlookers so that the place has the appearance of a busy corner.

About this same time the Promotion Society met to discuss:

Whether there should be any "laying of the cornerstone" in the new City Hall building, or whether no notice should be taken of the event until the "dedication" at the completion of the building.

Mr. Whitehurst, Mr. Fitzgerald and others favored having some ceremony at the laying of the cornerstone and placing in the stone a tin box containing a history of the event, records of the town, copies of the newspapers and other momentos. This would entail very little expense.

Mr. Roth and some others favored leaving all ceremonies until the completion of the building, but on motion of Mr. Whitehurst that the chair appoint a committee to arrange for the laying of the cornerstone the matter was carried.[30]

Wolfe was in frequent communication with the Council during the construction period, travelling down from San Jose to view the works and supervise the contractor. The matter of adding a heater in the basement for the fire engine was referred to committee. The question of a cornerstone was discussed and "the Mayor expressed himself as opposed to the names of the Mayor and Council appearing on same as being in bad taste." The Buildings and Grounds Committee was instructed to confer with the Promotion Committee "and arrange a suitable inscription." The Council also decided that the City vault should be downstairs rather than on the second floor, as originally planned, "provided there will be no additional expense to the city." One particularly happy change came when Wolfe informed the Council that the contractor had expressed a "willingness to trim all the openings of the second story of said building with sandstone instead of brick, without extra charge...."[31]

WE WILL REMEMBER MONDAY: Cornerstone and Dedication

"We will remember Monday... and the laying of the cornerstone of the City Hall," noted the *Gazette*. "It was an event that we had long hoped for and an occasion the like of which will not occur again in Gilroy during the present generation." On November 20th, after many months of anticipation, a photograph of almost generic perfection showed a scene of Americana dear to the hearts of painters two generations before and Norman Rockwell decades later. In the background the stone walls with arched openings stand a story high. In the center is a tripod of poles from which hangs the traditional cornerstone itself. To both sides are the citizens–men in hats, women in long skirts and full-sleeved shirts, and in the foreground is a white mongrel dog, happy to be a part of the historic moment. The *Gazette* described the event:

The streets on both fronts of the City Hall were crowded almost beyond conception for this city, with school pupils and citizens of both sexes on foot and in carriages. At a little past 2 o'clock the Gilroy Brass Band marched to the School Houses in accordance to a previously arranged programme, and from thence escorted the children of the High School and Grammar School to the corner of

Monterey and Sixth Streets where the crowd quickly gathered.

On a platform in the angle of the building were the prominent officers of the City Council and Promotion Society. Dr. Thayer, Chairman of the joint Committee called the company to order and remarked that as the day was blustering he would not make a lengthy introduction but would call on the children for a song.[1]

After speeches and more music, Mayor Dunlap concluded with the observation that "we have all we need in this beautiful valley, health, money, climate, and everything else to make us happy, now let us spend some of that money for public improvement (great applause)." At this point:

The cornerstone was then lowered into place by Councilman Seay. The tin box handed down by Clerk Hoover was placed within the stone and sealed up, the band played a patriotic selection and all the people sang America. The Rev. McKnight then pronounced the benediction and closed the ceremonies.

The laying of the cornerstone was widely seen as

Opposite:

Laying the City Hall Cornerstone,
November 20, 1905.
The Gilroy Museum

Under Construction. The City Hall 1906.
The Gilroy Museum

the culmination of a long and sometimes frustrating process, but, of course, the building was not yet anywhere near complete. In the middle of Janueary, 1906, citizens were reported to be "scared" by cracks in the brick walls. The Mayor quickly summoned architect Wolfe from San Jose, who reassured the town that after heavy rains the soil had settled "not more than one half inch." He left instructions for its repair and the Mayor announced that as soon as the weather permitted, crews would "have the building raised and the foundation leveled, and additionally strengthened by pillars underneath." The cost, he assured the city, would not exceed $100.[2]

AWFUL CATASTROPHE: The Quake of 1906

If the citizens were scared by the cracks caused by settling, they could hardly have anticipated the effect of the great earthquake of 1906. On April 18th the San Andreas fault shifted with devastating power, and much of the north central coast of California from Eureka to Salinas was damaged including, most famously and tragically, San Francisco. Three days later the *Gilroy Advocate* reported under the headline "Awful Catastrophe!" that "nearly every windmill between Gilroy and San Jose is down," and that while "nearly every chimney in town is down," the "damage was light and no lives lost." Significantly, while "many predicted that the City Hall would be flat, ...it stood the test admirably, losing only a little of the stone veneer, and some plastering inside." The previous day the *Gilroy Gazette* had more accurately informed the town that "the stone facings of the building on Sixth Street fell in considerable quantity. The metal coping on the south east corner of the building was wrenched off, and the plaster in the vestibule also knocked down."[1]

The City immediately retained Wolfe to aid the City Council committee that was to inspect buildings for damage. Two weeks later the City received an estimate of $1,050, and Wolfe was asked to comment on this as well. The Granite Rock Company was given the go-ahead to begin repairs, and on May 18th the newspaper reported that "most of the stone facings on Sixth Street will have to be re-set. The firewalls in places will have to be rebuilt and the ornamental finishings replaced."[2]

The bill for earthquake repairs was paid in June, and the City returned to the job of finishing off the building. At the end of the month the *Gazette* noticed that "steps have been laid in cement at the entrance door to the new City Hall. This gives it the appearance now of being soon ready for occupancy." The next month "the question regarding color of the paint to be used at the City Hall was left with the Committee on Buildings and Grounds" of the Council. The *Gazette* must have sent its art critic to check on the committee's work, because it announced that:

The City Hall is being painted, and the man who mixed the color that is being used, for a terra cotta tint, which it was reported that the metal work was to receive, must have had a very dark night of it before he commenced the work. It is to be hoped that the sun will fade the tint considerably, for at present it is simply hideous.[3]

The City Council meeting of September 14, 1906, was full of reports and decisions concerning the new building. Wolfe and McKenzie made a report, the Committee on Buildings and Grounds was "instructed to select color for tinting the stained walls in the front part of hall and work to be done by the contractors free of charge," the building was accepted and the contractors promised their $5,000. Mr. White was "instructed to see that the openings where the clock is to be placed be properly covered to prevent damage by rain," Mr. Wilson of the Granite Rock Company volunteered to check on insurance for the building, and then the matter of moving in was discussed. A committee on furnishings was appointed, and Mayor Dunlap along with Council members Princevalle and Milias were appointed "a general committee of arrangements in charge of the banquet and ball to be given upon the opening of the new City Hall."[4]

The *Advocate* gave details concerning the move to the new building: "It was decided," according to the reporter, "to use the building at once. The city marshal, clerk and engineer were appointed to arrange to move the fire department apparatus and furniture into the building, and Mayor Dunlap, Princevalle and Milias were authorized to arrange a banquet and ball for an opening which may help to furnish the assembly room with a suitable table and with desks and chairs for the council, clerk and newspaper reporters, the latter should not be overlooked."[5]

The arrangements for the banquet-ball fund-raiser were elaborate. The date was set for October 20th, and committees were established for the banquet (with a subcommittee on decorations), invitations, reception, and floor. Various prominent citizens, both men and women, were pressed into service, though the Council kept the key Invitation Committee exclusively to itself. Furthermore, "it was decided to charge $5 per couple, and gentlemen with more than one lady $2.50 extra for each additional lady. All proceeds to go toward the expense of furnishing the new hall." The *Gazette* responded with a veiled note of caution:

The very unusual spectacle of a Municipality giving an entertainment for the purpose of raising funds in order to place furniture in the vacant rooms of the imposing $20,000 building before it can be of any service had led to a number of comments and inquiries. As it is a public matter all the people seem to have taken an interest in the affair and want to know something more about the proceedings. There is evidently a diversity of opinions from the number of inquiries and suggestions which have come to the Gazette. As some of the plans, perhaps all of them, are subject to change....[6]

It is possible that the $5 per couple ticket price to the event revealed a little too clearly that the town's

The Gilroy Museum

elite was, as was often the case, handling the affairs of the community in a manner which kept some other citizens in a less participatory role. The plans, possibly subjected to a groundswell of democratic objection, may well have been changed. Neither of the city's newspapers reported any ball or banquet

in the days after the announced date.

Meanwhile, the Council proceeded to move into the building, even if it was not yet properly furnished. The meeting of October 1st was the first to be held in the City Hall. "The room used by the tax collector," according to the *Advocate*, "in the basement at the east end of the building was furnished and lighted by electricity specifically for this service.... The Marshal's room at the new City Hall was a comfortable Chamber for the Board and the usual visitors who interested themselves sufficiently in municipal affairs to attend the meeting."[7]

The use of the new building did not cause old problems to go away. The promise of the City to pay off the Granite Rock Company was easier made than fulfilled. A gentle reminder by the contractor early in December brought the revelation that land which the City had hoped to sell to pay the bill was as yet unsold, and the contractors were asked for an extension. A week later the City decided to pay, but only after the "matter of leaks in roof be considered."[8] Not until July 1907 were the Granite Rock Company and the architects Wolfe and McKenzie finally paid. The newspapers proclaimed "City Hall Free From Debt."[9]

Nor did the furnishings problem prove easily solved. The *Advocate* charged "we have a spacious assembly room in the main city hall, bare of furniture and unoccupied. This room should be the pride of the town. It belongs to the people. Twenty-five thousand dollars of their money is in it. Let it be opened for use." The public and promotional nature of the building would be emphasized:

There is not only ample room for the pictures of the city fathers and mothers, but also for exhibits of the valley products, to attract the eyes of visitors. The room should be furnished with tables, chair, newspaper racks, writing desks...[10]

In July 1907, five months later, the Council's Buildings and Grounds Committee was instructed to "take up the matter of furnishing the City Hall and render report as soon as convenient." When the report was made a week later it was decided to go out for bids on the needed items. The bids were opened on August 12th, and the choice between them was left up to the committee which picked that of C.F. Weber & Company.[11]

Meanwhile in August, the Council authorized the Promotion Club to draw $200 from the city's coffers "toward securing the proper furnishings for a room in the City Hall to be used as a place for a permanent display of farm products." The grant was conditional, however, on the Club working with the Council in picking out the right furnishings. The Mayor thought that $50 of the $200 should go toward providing a glass case at the Southern Pacific Railroad depot, but it was not a formal condition.[12]

Finally, the furnishings were in place. On October 7, 1907, nearly two years after the laying of the cornerstone and nearly a year to the day after having moved in, the City Council met for the first time in the main assembly hall.[13]

FOR THE RECEPTION OF BOOKS: The Library

Even before the laying of the cornerstone of the new City Hall, "a committee of ladies in the interests of the Promotion Society was present [at a Council meeting] and asked the Council to donate the present City Hall and Engine House property [on Fifth Street east of Eigleberry] for a site for a Public Library." Other citizens spoke for the plan as well, and "each of the Councilmen expressed themselves as being in accord with the plans."[1] A month later a petition was presented to the Council, signed by more than a quarter of the voters, asking that a Library Board be set up. The Promotion Society again spoke in favor of the measure, and were perhaps responsible for the presence at the meeting of a representative from the State Library in Sacramento. The librarian "informed the Council that it was mandatory for them to act in the matter." It was referred to the Ordinance Committee, and in January 1906, the new board was established.[2]

In February, the Library Board officially requested the Council to donate the original City Hall/Engine House site for a public library, but once again the matter was "laid over for further consideration." A year later, the *Advocate*, in calling for the proper furnishing of the new City Hall, suggested that this might include "glass cases for the reception of books; or," it continued sarcastically, "has the city expectations of a Carnegie library?"[3] Failing to get either their own site or building, the City's Library Board finally asked, in August 1907, "for the use of a room in the City Hall and three-fours of a mill as a special tax for library purposes."[4] Such space was eventually granted in the new building and added to the expansion of services available at the site. A year later, the foresight of the *Advocate* was proved. On December 7, 1908, the City accepted $10,000 from Andrew Carnegie for a separate library building.[5]

MARVELOUSLY BAROQUE: Architect and Style

The building has, over the years, proved difficult to describe with accuracy and consistency. From the time the first drawings were put on display, it was said by some that it was to look like the 1892 U.S. Post Office building in San Jose. Built of sandstone, it has been described as a "Richardson Romanesque structure"[1] and, since 1970, it has housed the San Jose Museum of Art.

The City Hall, on the other hand, was described, perhaps somewhat reluctantly, by the same scholar as Mission Revival. It is claimed in the same place that the real architect of the hall was the prominent California designer, Samuel Newsom. Despite the fact that the daring and dramatic building does suggest Newsom's hand, no documentation connecting him with the structure is known to exist.[2] Another writer called it a "marvelously baroque" building, the city's "only one outstanding piece of architecture" and a guide book refers to it as the basis of "Gilroy's fame."[3] Other popular labels have included "a gingerbread house with gables," the "Indonesian Pagoda of Gilroy," and "the be-gabled, be-portholed, be-turreted structure."[4] However, to most Gilroyans, perhaps, the building's style is known simply and somewhat mysteriously as "Flemish" or "Flemish baroque."

Opposite:

Gilroy City Hall. A Retouched Postcard View, c.1906.
Lake County Museum: Curt Teich Postcard Collection

PROCLAIMING THE FLIGHT OF TIME: The Tower Clock and Bell

As early as March, 1906, the matter of the clock for the City Hall tower was occupying the minds of the Mayor and City Council. On March 13th, in a Council meeting, Mayor Dunlap "informed the Council that a subscription was being taken up for the purchase of a four dial clock for the New City Hall to cost about $700.00 and that the list was left with the Bank of Gilroy." The wealthy rancher and landowner Henry Miller gave $100 to the fund, the Mayor himself put in $50, and $50 was also received from L.A. Whitehurst. Then, apparently, the fund languished.[1]

Nothing further appeared in the Council minutes concerning the clock until late in 1913 permission was granted to H.J. Musgrave, of San Francisco, to install a Seth Thomas Tower Clock, with four dials, in the City Hall tower. The Council formally washed its hands of any expenses which might arise from the clock or its installation and forced Musgrave to agree "to keep all rain and moisture from entering said tower through any opening made by him." The press drew the obvious conclusion that a clock was somewhere in the offing, but declared that the name of the "donor is a profound secret."[2]

Finally in February, the clock was unveiled and the donor named. The *Advocate* announced:

The handsome town clock installed this week in the tower of the city hall has excited the admiration of our citizens. The name of the donor was to be kept a profound secret, but it has become generally known that Mrs. Caroline A. Hoxett is the town's fairy god-mother.... Nothing could be more useful to the city for years to come, than this handsome clock, which will mark the passing of the hours....[3]

The formal presentation of the clock by Mrs. Hoxett to the City took place on March 2, 1914. In response, the Council passed an eloquent resolution praising civic pride, the public good, and the donor's record of generosity to the town (which also included the land for the Carnegie Library building and the I.O.O.F. Children's Home). The clock itself was praised as well, with its hands that "will ever point the hour and its bell, at stated intervals, proclaim the flight of time." Finally, it proclaimed Mrs. Hoxett Gilroy's "most public spirited citizen."[4] The new bell was installed sometime afterwards.

The City Hall's clock became its symbol for many people, both locals and those from out-of-town. For people passing through Gilroy on the main north-south highway, it was a useful landmark, as well as an image of Gilroy that would easily spring to mind later. For some Gilroy residents, it was a habitual reference point. Mary Prien recalls the clock as a

Caroline A. Hoxett   *The Gilroy Museum*

strong image of her girlhood. It was associated with returning home via Sixth Street, after a shopping trip to town with her mother; they would note the time on the clock as they left and thus figure out their schedule for supper. It also was important on her route to school on the schoolbus; she recalls always checking on the way to school in the morning to see if they were late.[5]

The Old City Hall clock was designed to operate by a pendulum. It was wound with a crank, much like the crank for a Model T, and a brass key was used to move the hands on all four clock faces. The speed of the clock was adjusted with a brass knob.[6]

Access to the tower was through the judge's office upstairs; there were 46 stairs to the clock machinery room, 35 feet above street level. Nancy McCarthy, a long-time Gilroy newspaper reporter, recalls how the judge kept huge stacks of papers and books in his chambers, making access even more difficult.[7] The last thirteen steps narrow, and the passageway became somewhat treacherous. Ladders to the clock faces, 12 feet higher, and the belltower, another eight feet above that, were even more threatening.

The bell in the clocktower had two purposes. It automatically sounded the hourly (and half-hourly) chime when a hammerhead striker hit the bell's exterior, but the bell could also be rung manually. For this purpose, long ropes hung from the belltower through the clock room down to the building's main doors. This warning bell system was used by the City's volunteer fire department before the new station was built in 1916. The bell was also sounded for special events. Gilroyans easily recognized the difference in sound between the hourly strike and the manual ring.

For many years the clock's maintenance (oiling, etc.) was done by the Lawtons of Lawton's Gem Store Inc. Mrs. Elizabeth Lawton recalls her husband George working on the clock back in the 1930s. She especially recalls that he complained that it was hard to get up there to do anything on it: the access stairs through the judge's office weren't easily reached or easy to climb. Their son Philip took over the cleaning of the clock from his father. Philip Lawton described the winding as being awkward, because there was little room in the belfry, and the cables were so long that it took a long time to wind them.[8]

In the late 1960s, when the Gilroy Historical Society leased the building, Paul Scheck, owner of Paul's Trading Post next door to the Old City Hall, wound the clock every day. After Scheck's retirement, Charles Gilmore, Sr., installed an electric motor to the clockworks. Volunteer winders were no longer required, except at daylight saving time, when they would adjust and oil it at the same time.[9]

When the building was being refurbished in 1980 by Hoffman and Associates, the pendulum works were restored as a part of the building's historic restoration. During the Hoffman years, Ralph Blackburn, the owner/resident of Gilroy Hardware across the street, voluntarily wound the clock. His interest was aroused when Gene Corriden, a Santa Cruz specialist hired by the Hoffmans to restore the clock, came into Gilroy Hardware to buy parts. Blackburn attended to the clock twice a week.[10]

During the demise of the Hoffmans' business, however, Blackburn quit over a dispute, and other disgruntled employees vandalized the clockworks, leaving it, and later the building, to be overrun by pigeons and stray cats. In 1986, Corriden again restored the clock with handmade parts, and Gilroy City employee Chuck Myer took on the responsibility of winding and maintaining the clockworks. Later, employees of the Old City Hall Restaurant, first under the management of Fred Lombardi and then under Russ Hendrickson, became the logical ones for the job.

Closely associated with the clock in the minds of many Gilroyans have been the flocks of pigeons which installed their roosts in the belfry. The mess which goes with pigeons, like smoke goes with fire, was plain for all to see on the clocktower as well as on the front steps of the building. Al Gagliardi recalls that clean up became one of the continuing chores of the police officers. Sometimes the officers themselves would sweep and wash the City Hall's front steps as part of their routine chores.

Ralph Blackburn, owner of
Gilroy Hardware, winds the City
Hall clock in 1984.

The Gilroy Dispatch

Sometimes trusted prisoners were given the task, which could then be taken into consideration by the judge as part of their sentence. The police officers would occasionally go up into the clock tower and catch a few pigeons and remove some eggs, but the problem was never solved. In the late 1960s, the Gilroy Historical Society, then lease-holders of the building, scared the pigeons off with an owl and some mice.[11]

One thing which temporarily disturbed the contented roost of the pigeons had been the hourly ringing of the bell: each time there would be a flurry of pigeons scattering. The bell was silenced due to complaints from local residents and guests at the Milias Hotel across the street that it was keeping them awake at night. The bell tolled out at least one moment of history: Frances Howson Vigna recalls that her brother, Lawrence Cullen, seven years old, was held aloft on the shoulders of their father and some other men of the town to reach the bell-rope and toll out the joyous news of the Armistice, on November 11, 1918, as soon as the news reached town.

The smooth operation of the City Hall clock was disturbed at least twice by major earthquakes. The ticking of the clock was stopped by the 1959 earthquake, Judge John Klarich recalls.[12] For some time after the quake, the clock stood in mute testimony to the time it had hit, just as it would again thirty years later. After the October 17, 1989 quake, the image of 5:04 p.m., frozen in the minds of all who experienced the temblor, was also frozen on the face of the clock into 1991.

THOUSANDS WILL PASS THROUGH OUR CITY:
Improving Monterey Street

The completion of the new City Hall did indeed, as intended, call attention to the spirit and status of the City of Gilroy. It also drew the attention of citizens and travelers alike to the condition of Monterey Street. The main thoroughfare of the town was still unpaved, and was frequently used for driving herds of cattle and flocks of sheep through town. It lacked sidewalks, and was lined with telephone and electrical utility poles. In 1912, the State of California voted $18 million worth of bonds for highway construction and improvement. This was the birth of the State's integrated highway system. Alarmed at rumors that the major north-south route would traverse Santa Clara Valley along a mountain rather than a mid-valley route, the City Council was prompted to act. If El Camino Real would pass from San Francisco to San Juan Bautista, the Council pledged to "cause to be constructed through the City of Gilroy so as to complete said highway a street that will be equal in every way to the roadway to be constructed by the

Opposite:

Preparing to pave Monterey Street in 1913, view looking north.
The Gilroy Museum

State Highway Commissiion."[1]

The urge to get the state highway to run through the middle of town was based as much on economics, no doubt, as on pride. In the dawning age of the automobile, the tourist was seen as a desirable source of income by many communities. A year after the initial appeal, the Gilroy Chamber of Commerce and the Women's Civic Club both petitioned the City Council to pave Monterey Street to a width of 24 feet through the entire town, from city limit to city limit. The Council responded by resolving that "the public interest and necessity demands the acquisition, construction and completion of" the paving of Monterey Street. The cost was estimated at $34,806, or nearly $12,000 more than the normal yearly income of the city.[2] A bond election was held, and the necessary funds were voted late in May, 1913.[3] A year later, the *Advocate* noted that "our citizens are rejoicing over the completion of the Monterey street pavement.... It is one of the finest streets in the state, and being on the State highway, thousands will pass through our city."[4]

There was no logical end to civic pride, of course. First there was the magnificent City Hall, then the paving of the highway past its front door. Even

before this was completed, the Council took action to require the telephone company to remove its poles along Monterey Street, and either bury them in "a cable underground" or run them up a parallel alley. A few years later, it was deemed necessary to lay a sidewalk along the north side of Sixth Street, between Monterey Street and the railroad right-of-way.[5] At last the City Hall had the sort of modern municipal amenities which the building demanded and deserved.

HEATED RIVALRY: The Volunteer fire Companies

One of the important original uses of the new City Hall was as the new home of the Gilroy Volunteer Fire department. In fact, the city had two volunteer fire companies, and there was considerable rivalry between them. On October 3, 1904, before a shovel full of dirt had been moved for the new building, the Vigilant Engine Company objected to "the grouping of all the fire apparatus in one building...."[1] The company's reasoning was that "property in general, and particularly in the northern part of the City, would be better protected if the apparatus were housed in buildings separated by some distance, as is the case at present, and...we believe there is a likelihood of serious danger from confusion or possible collision in housing the apparatus of the whole Department, in the same building..."[2]

Opposite:

Monterey Street during the 1920s, looking south. On the left side is the Central Hotel (present site of Penney's), the Bank of Gilroy (today a parking lot), the I.O.O.F. Building (later Wells Fargo Bank). *The Gilroy Museum*

It appears that the Vigilant Company stood fast by its objections and continued to keep its equipment at its old firehouse. In the Fall of 1906, however, it formed a committee to meet with the Eureka Hook and Ladder Company, its competitor, to jointly "arrange the meeting room at the New City Hall."[3] Meanwhile the Eureka Company moved with eagerness. Its records noted that February 4, 1907 "was the last meeting to be held in the old Truck-house and in the future the Company would meet in the New City Hall...." One of its last items of business in the old quarters was to "present the carpet on the floor" to John Rea, one of its members. That same day the Council instructed the Superintendent of Lighting to "see that the proper connections were made for lighting the Firemen's meeting room," and the next meeting, held on March 7, was proudly logged in as being in the "City Hall."[4]

In May 1908, the reluctant Vigilant Company finally began to hold its own meetings in the City Hall and four months later the Eureka Company appointed a committee "to see about repairing the bell and removing it to the rear of City Hall." The committee reported that the old bell was beyond repair and early in 1909, the Eureka voted that the

Chief should "call a special meeting of both companies for the purpose of making arrangements for the giving of a ball to raise funds for the purpose of buying a bell and building a tower for same." In May the company put $10 in the bell fund, bringing the total to $190, voted to make the purchase, and asked the City Council to erect a freestanding tower in which to hang it (there being no bell or clock yet in the main belltower). A new fire bell arrived in November, and was erected outside near the rear of the building.[5]

Although it appears that the Vigilant Company, while keeping its equipment at the old truck-house, was now meeting in the City Hall, and the Eureka Company had moved both its equipment and meeting place there. Worry over the accommodations continued for a surprising number of years. In January 1909, the Council admitted that "$150 would be required to make the lower floor of City Hall serviceable for fire apparatus." In January of 1910, just two days after the Council accepted an invitation to "attend opening night at Vigilant Engine Company's newly furnished headquarters," the Eureka Company formed a committee to "interview the city council about securing the room now occupied by library for the use of this Company."[6]

Finally, in March of the next year the Council voted the $150 to properly furnish the Eureka meeting room. The members of the Eureka Company were grateful, and over the next few years allowed such community groups as the Ladies Civic Club and the Merchants' Association to use their facility for meeting purposes.[7]

The fact that half the Gilroy Fire Department was housed a few blocks distant from the City Hall was clearly problematic since the City had two, not one, firehouses. Then during the Winter of 1915-16, the Council spent $5,000 on a new American La France "Chemical Auto Engine." The *Advocate* carried a picture of the machine under the heading "Gilroy's Latest Addition to Fire Department Equipment," and revealed that it was being "kept at the Tice Garage."[8] It seems likely that the engine was considered too big for the City Hall facility, or that the latter was already crowded, because in February, 1916, the City Council contracted with the architect William Binder to "draw the plans and specifications for the new firehouse."[9]

According to the *Advocate*, the building was to be:

A two-story re-inforced concrete building to be erected on the city's lot on Fifth street, now occupied by the Vigilant Engine Co. and old city hall and jail. The building is to be used to house the handsome new chemical engine and other fire apparatus down stairs, and the second story will be used for club and meeting room for the firemen and for sleeping quarters for the engineer, chief and other firemen who will be on duty at any hour of the night to man

GILROY'S LATEST ADDITION TO
FIRE DEPARTMENT EQUIPMENT

American La France Chemical Aut> Engine Gives General Satisfaction

The *Gilroy Advocate* proudly announced this
addition to the city's fire department,
March 25, 1916.
The Gilroy Museum

the new engine. The new building will cost in the neighborhood of $5000.[10]

Plans and specifications for the new firehouse were accepted in March of 1916, and the next month the bid of William Radtke to build the structure for $5,853 also was accepted.[11] On the same night in September, the Eureka Company noted somewhat tersely that they heard "remarks from the chief and others spoke about the new fire quarters," and the Vigilant Company appointed a committee to work with the Eurekas on "the necessary preparations for the returning to our new home."[12] A month later each company donated $100 toward "furnishing the new club room," and in November, the Vigilant group was able to report the "purchase of a pool table, rugs and electrical fixtures." The old rugs were donated to the city.[13] In December, the *Gilroy Advocate* reported on the festive first meeting of the two companies in their new home. Five new members were initiated, and "the boys were put over the jumps in a most

Opposite:

Gilroy's first paid driver, Shirley Johnson, and Otto Homlein with the Vigilant Engine Company's steam pumper at the Fifth Street Fire House, c. 1917. *The Gilroy Museum*

thrilling initiatory ceremony." The paper noted that:

The club rooms will be open at all times for the members of both companies. A movement is on foot to consolidate both companies into one big strong company. The day of rivalry is over, and what the city wants is efficiency. The club room is equipped with pool and card tables, and will prove a good home for the young men about town to while away a pleasant evening. After the speeches light refreshments were served.[14]

The City Hall was now free of the need for sloped floors, fire poles and fire doors. After the engines were transferred to their new quarters, offices took their place downstairs in City Hall.

Now that both companies were sharing the same new quarters (something that had never happened in the City Hall building) and both the equipment and service were being upgraded, it was increasingly evident that the long term rivalry no longer served any purpose. On December 7, 1921, the Vigilant Engine Company resolved that it was "for the best interests of said Fire Department that all Companies of said Department to be consolidated into one Company." On February 10, 1922, the Eureka Hook and Ladder Company passed a similar resolution, declaring that "the two company [sic] be formed into one to be known as the Gilroy Volunteer Fire Company." The merger was accomplished.[15]

37

PALM TREE AND FLAGPOLE: Facade and Accoutrements

The facade of the City Hall has been characterized by different features at different times, such as the striped awning over an upstairs front window which is shown in an early 1910s view of the building. At the time that it was built, and during the following years, there was a flagpole on the corner close to the front steps. George White remembers that his grandfather, Constable John White, used to tell a story that took place just after the building opened. One of the town characters climbed to the top of the flagpole, clung to the revolving weathervane at the top and refused to budge. The Marshal, failing to coax the man to come down, came and asked Constable White, who had some acquaintance with the man, to help. Constable White scaled the flagpole himself and managed to talk the man down.[1]

The flagpole was later cropped and used as a telegraph or telephone pole. Later it was removed altogether. A palm tree was planted alongside the City Hall on the Sixth Street side, probably in the 1910s, and had become quite sizable by the time it was removed in 1925.[2]

The facade of the City Hall was featured during city events. During the 1920s and 1930s, when Memorial Day and Independence Day parades were staged, the reviewing stands were usually located close to the City Hall. Mary Prien recalls that her family, excitedly coming to town to enjoy these parades, would always try to secure a place close to the City Hall, between Martin Street and Sixth Street, so that they could hear the descriptions of the events. Later on, the high school band, which was particularly renowned for its excellence in the 1930s and 1940s, would march up and down Monterey Street past the City Hall.[3]

Opposite:

A palm tree added decoration to the City Hall during the 1910s and 1920s, and the Chamber of Commerce had an exhibit of local products on the first floor facing Monterey Street.
The Gilroy Museum

Fourth of July Parade around 1920 moves north along Monterey Street.

MATRONS, MARSHALS, POLICE AND SHERIFF: Law Enforcement

George White's grandfather, Constable John E. White, worked in the City Hall from the opening of the building until his death in office in 1936. As Constable, he was an officer of the County rather than the City; there were two constables and a nightwatchman on staff. If he needed help, he would call in someone from the Sheriff's office. He had a small desk in the corner of the City Marshal's office, which was next door to the jail, at the eastern end of the building.[1] The City Marshal was later renamed Chief of Police during the 1960 charter revision.

Virginia Cox recalls the office vividly, having worked as Police Matron from 1930 to 1932, when Walter S. White, John White's son, was City Marshal and Judge Leon Thomas ran the Gilroy Justice Court. In 1932, she was transferred to San Jose where she stayed for ten years. In 1943, she was called in to the Gilroy office to help out while another matron, Louise Shell, was sick. Temporary became permanent, and she stayed until she retired in the early 1960s, after having worked for City Marshal Harold Sturla.[2]

As Police Matron, her job was primarily at the radio, dispatching police officers. She was the only one doing that, so when she went to lunch or had

to accompany one of the officers, another officer had to take over the radio. One of her duties was to be present anytime that a police officer was dealing with a woman charged or arrested. This meant that she was on call even at home, and was occasionally called out of bed at night to go and be present at an arrest.

Since there were few women prisoners, this part of the Police Matron's job did not occupy the majority of her time. When there was a woman prisoner, however, she would also have to accompany the prisoner up to the courtroom and stay with her throughout the trial, and when the woman was in her cell, the matron would be present anytime an officer took her any food or drink. Virginia Cox enjoyed her job enormously and felt that the police officers were "good as gold" to her. She was the only woman working in that office, so she shared all the facilities with the men, whom she said were "just perfect."

The office in which she worked was small, with one window and a door going back to the jail. Virginia Cox is especially fond of the Old City Hall for a further reason: she and Phil Cox, the City Clerk, were married by Judge Thomas in the Judge's office there. After the ceremony, she recalls, the wedding party came down the double curved staircase at the front of the building, and crossed the street to the Milias Hotel.[3] Carol Cassell later replaced Cox as Police Matron.

Different citizens of Gilroy have experienced the police station in the Old City Hall in a variety of ways. Mayor Roberta Hughan, had the experience of seeing the police station from the inside when she and about seventeen other high school seniors were taken down to the station for a Halloween prank in 1949. The thing to do for Halloween, apparently, was to get in the back of a pickup and tour the streets of Gilroy throwing tomatoes at people in the back of other pickups. Unfortunately, the Gilroy police weren't in on the joke; they took all eighteen of them down to the station. Rather than arresting them, the officers let them cool their heels while they called their parents. There was no way they could have dealt with all eighteen offenders overnight, even if they had thought the offense that serious. However, the group, which included most of the student body officers at the high school that year, did have to go back twice for court appearances in which they were soundly lectured by the judge.[4]

The Sheriff's substation, for at least some time, was not located in the City Hall itself, but across the street at Broderson's Buick garage, where the Highway Patrol was also located.[5]

PROPER TOILET AND SANITARY BEDS: The Jail

Perhaps there were few offenders needing incarceration, or the provision of a new jail in the City Hall was simply not a high priority when the City Hall was first built. In December 1907, the Lighting Committee of the City Council was still concerned with arranging for the new jail to be cleaned and placed in "proper shape."[1] In May, 1909, the Buildings and Grounds Committee was instructed to see about placing a "proper toilet" in the jail at the new City Hall.[2] In December, 1912, the question of a toilet and water in the jail came up again,[3] and in February 1918 the question of "sanitary beds" was discussed. The Board of Charities and Corrections notified the City Council that they were satisfied with the conditions in the jail except for the beds. They were not happy with the board beds provided, and recommended that "sanitary wall beds be installed."[4]

Even when the inside of the jail was finally in shape, the outside was often the subject of local attention. Frances Cullen Howson Vigna recalls that, when she was a child, if she had to walk down Sixth Street, she would cross over and walk down the other side because the prisoners in the jail frightened her. "They would climb up to the barred windows slightly above their heads, and yell so that you'd think they might get through even when you knew they really couldn't."[5] A generation later, her daughter, Roberta Howson Hughan remembers that, when she was a child, they would drive by the jail and there would be a group of prisoners' wives or friends congregated on the sidewalk outside the cells on Sixth Street, having informal visiting hours. The prisoners and their wives couldn't see each other, because the windows are above eye level, but they could talk or yell back and forth.[6]

Albert Gagliardi worked as a Sheriff's Deputy for some years while the police and the jail were in the Old City Hall. The jail was just a holding facility. The serious cases would be sent up to the criminal court at San Jose. This meant that there were no jailers in Gilroy, and the Sheriff's deputies would have to check on any prisoners in the cells. The jail was a confined one, consisting of a big cell, a small cell, a "ladies' cell," and one where they could keep juveniles temporarily. (This was before the law changed such that all juveniles had to go to special facilities.) The "ladies' cell" was small and had an iron door for the sake of privacy, whereas the other cells had iron bars on the doors.

Occasionally, Gagliardi recalls, the deputies would have trouble with the prisoners, such as one of them setting fire to the mattress (of a "sanitary bed"), and the deputies would have to get all the prisoners out. Prisoners were never held for more than several days; cases requiring longer sentences went to San Jose. He also remembers that he and the other deputies would go and get the food for the prisoners twice a day, from "Ray's Lunch" halfway down the block where they had a charge account. They would get the same thing for each prisoner for breakfast and for dinner: hamburger and french fries. They would also get an old metal coffee-pot full of coffee. The offenses for which people landed in the Gilroy jail were mostly drunken driving and other misdemeanors.[7]

Judge Leon Thomas
The Gilroy Museum

LIKE THE WILD WEST: Gilroy's Justice Court

In the late 19th century, state law in California provided that each incorporated city might elect or appoint its own police judge. According to Judge Mark Thomas of the Santa Clara County Court, "the police judge could hear only petty misdemeanors and drunk cases occurring within the city, while the justice of the peace could also handle preliminary felony proceedings and civil cases. As recently as 1976, there was no requirement that the police or justice court judge be a licensed attorney."[1] From 1850 onwards, Gilroy usually had two justices of the peace, both of whom doubled as police judges. The court in Gilroy was a Justices' Court, part of the Santa Clara County court system.

When the court opened in the new City Hall in 1906, Howard Willey and John Baillaige were the two justices. Howard Willey served an extraordinary thirty-six years in office. It was during Willey's term in office that the number of justices was reduced to one, probably before 1914, and the City Council appointed him "Police Judge for the City of Gilroy for the ensuing year."[2] Willey, a man of apparent energy, was an accomplished gardener, and a correspondent for the *San Jose Mercury* for twelve years, and enjoyed a reputation for being well-read. He retired in January 1919.[3] His home on Fifth Street, known as a cultural center even then, is now under City ownership for that purpose. Willey was replaced by Judge John M. Hoesch, who had previously served as fire department engineer, plumbing and sewer inspector and superintendent of the water works.[4]

In the 1930 election, Hoesch was defeated by former manager of the Miller and Lux ranches, Leon Thomas, who was to "become a local fixture."[5] Virginia Cox, who, as Police Matron, had some official dealings with him from 1930-32 and 1943-58, recalls Judge Thomas as "a wonderful man."[6] Al Gagliardi, who became a sheriff's deputy in 1949, took prisoners before Judge Thomas as part of his routine duties. He recalls him as a colorful, comical character. Thomas would be direct and pointed towards the defendant, asking them things like, "Why don't you get a haircut?"

An enthusiastic member of the local Duck Club, Thomas would deal with the cases at hand rapidly, insisting that it needn't take long to find a defendant guilty, especially during duck-hunting season. Sometimes he did not even raise his eyes from the paperwork to look at the person in the dock. As might be expected, his verdicts were not always well received by the defendants. Once, a disgruntled defendant called the judge something like "an old codger," at which the Judge immediately removed his coat and began to spar around toward him, asking the deputies to open the gate and let him at him. Another time a defendant, less than happy with his verdict, sliced off one of the two bell-ropes from the stairwell on his way out.[7]

Patricia Baker began working as Court Clerk for Judge Thomas in 1954. She remembers him as a very colorful, old-fashioned judge who sometimes put his feet up on the desk while he arraigned people.[8] As Court Clerk, Patricia Baker did all the bookkeeping and paperwork associated with court business, including taking notes at trial proceedings. Occasionally she would need to look up old dockets, which would involve going up into the clocktower and hunting for them amidst the dust and the cobwebs. There were always two court clerks and the judge. The court was not full-time, but only one or two days a week.

When Gilroy and Morgan Hill were joined into one municipal judicial district in 1965, Patricia Baker became the first official Justice Court Clerk in California. Just as Virginia Cox, Police Matron, and Phil Cox, City Clerk, were a City Hall couple, so were Patricia Baker and her husband Bob, who was a Sergeant in the Police Department downstairs.

When Judge Thomas retired in 1958, his successor was Judge John M. Klarich, the first qualified attorney to hold the office in Gilroy. When Judge Klarich took over the Gilroy Justice Court, he brought a brisk professionalism with him. Baker described Judge Klarich as a quick, "brilliant" judge, emphasizing the speed and efficiency with which he worked.[9] Immediately he was dissatisfied with the courtroom, which he described as being like the Wild West, with only a bare lightbulb hanging from the ceiling, no proper set of lawbooks, and a constant mess made by the pigeons. Everyone agreed that the pigeons were a perennial nuisance, and Judge Klarich objected to the way they would mess up the courtroom by flying in the large, open windows, roosting in the rafters, and then getting scared every time a train went by. Some people, alert to the problem, would come to the courtroom armed with a towel. The pigeon problem did at least provide some comic relief in the middle of a court session, when they would fly in the window and everyone would duck.

Judge Klarich's conviction that the courtroom was inadequate was hardened in 1959 when an earthquake measuring 5.3 on the Richter scale cracked the walls, causing him to run out of the building and giving him the strong feeling that the building was not only functionally lacking, but also unsafe.[10] Not one to accept unsatisfactory conditions, Klarich began a move for better court facilities. Apart from anything else, he felt that the existing courtroom was inadequate because the judge had no privacy in which to talk to lawyers.

City Hall Jail Yard. A large whiskey still seized
by local officers during Prohibition, c. 1929-1930.

The Gilroy Museum

His office, in the front of the building with a window facing on to Monterey Street, was partitioned from the other rooms upstairs by a division rather than a proper wall. The two court clerks had a little room with no doors, and they could hear everything the judge said. All who remember the courtroom agree that it was quite basic, though functional: plain varnished wooden benches, a big desk for the judge, an ordinary table for the attorneys, and a chair for the bailiff. The walls were plain but painted.

One reason for the poor facilities, it seems, is that the Gilroy Court was supplied with all its equipment by the Santa Clara County Court offices in San Jose. It often received second-hand equipment when they had asked for new pieces, which seemed particularly unfair in view of the fact that the Gilroy Court brought in more than its share of the revenue.

In 1959, Judge Klarich opened a temporary courtroom in a storefront north along Monterey Street, in premises which had been the Gilroy Rubber Works and then a flower shop. Finally, Klarich's campaign for better court facilities came to fruition with the opening of the new courthouse at 50 South Rosanna Street on July 17, 1963. At the dedication ceremony on September 26, 1963, Judge Leon Thomas commented that it was the end of an era of inadequate facilities "after years of struggle with almost nothing to work with."[11] Klarich ended the "Wild West" era with an ironic footnote: he himself stepped down from the bench in 1973, the year he was found guilty of brandishing a weapon at a noisy Pacific Gas & Electric crew.[12]

HEADQUARTERS OF CIVILIAN DEFENSE: World War II

World War I had little impact on city administration in Gilroy. World War II, however, had various ramifications for the city, its officers, and for the City Hall. The registration of aliens began just after the war started. This affected many local Japanese-Americans, some of whom had been well-established local producers for decades. It also involved non-U.S. citizens of other nationalities: Italians, Germans, Filipinos, and others.

William Frassetti, Sr., was an employee of the Gilroy Post Office and was involved in registration of aliens. The location for registration varied, and the locations and times were advertised at the post office and in the local newspapers. Registration was held at the City Hall for about three weeks, upstairs in the large court and council meeting room. The registration would begin at 8 a.m. and would sometimes go until 11 p.m., although the officers would be relieved for meal breaks. The people being registered as aliens were fingerprinted and would have to fill out a form which included name, address, birthplace, family history and physical description. They were then presented with a book like a passport with their name, number, address, photograph and physical description.[1]

The City Hall was also the headquarters for the civilian defense organization in Gilroy. On Thursday, February 26, 1942, the *Gilroy Advocate* reported that the civilian defense headquarters in the City Hall announced that "Wednesday would be the last day for volunteer transportation workers to secure identification cards" and that all workers on the committee had been notified that the cards were waiting for them. Arm bands for civilian defense workers were being issued at City Hall, as well.[2] The Red Cross also used the City Hall in their defense efforts. For instance, on Thursday, June 11, 1942, the *Gilroy Advocate* reported that "Red Cross first aid workers met Friday night at City Hall and heard Phil Cox, executive head of the local defense council, and Robert H. Bates, head of the Red Cross, outline the work expected of them and other civilian defense workers during a blackout or air raid."

Besides housing these defense organizations, the City Hall became the venue for at least one event held to rally citizens' support for the war effort. On November 19, 1942, the City Hall was the backdrop for the "Tojo Cigar," a Japanese two-man submarine which had been captured by American forces at Oahu Island. Weeks before the event, the *Gilroy Advocate* advertised the forthcoming appearance of

"Tojo Cigar" at the Gilroy City Hall on November 19, 1942.

The Gilroy Museum

"America's first prize of war," claiming that the submarine "designed as a suicide ship and a secret weapon by the little yellow men will be launched by the U.S. Treasury Department, and patriotic Americans will remember Pearl Harbor, Manila, Guam, Wake Island and Corregidor by buying War Bonds and Stamps."[3] Plenty of patriotic Americans in Gilroy responded to the *Advocate's* call. On November 25, 1942, reporting on this early stop in a nationwide war bond selling tour of the "Tojo Cigar," the pictures in the *Advocate* showed a thronging crowd, with war bond stamps being pasted on the side of the submarine to spell "Gilroy."

Mrs. Ed Avery was in charge of pasting war bond stamps on the submarine, while Richard K. Whitmore chaired the community event.
The Gilroy Museum

THE HUB OF AFFAIRS: City Administration

An essential function of the City Hall, naturally, was to house the administrative offices of the City, such as the City Clerk's office and the Water Department where people would go to pay their water bills. In 1949, the city administration, which was downstairs and toward the front of the building, consisted of the city clerk, the assistant city clerk, the city treasurer and the building inspector.

Two men filled the top slot during the building's first half-century. Eugene F. Rogers was elected to sixteen terms as City Clerk between 1906 and 1937, when he died in office. His deputy, Phil A. Cox, took over for another two decades until he, too, died in office on June 23, 1957. Deputy Clerk Graydon B. Carr assumed leadership, and in 1960 assumed the new title of City Administrator after the charter was revised. At that point, Susanne Thomas (Steinmetz) was named City Clerk, and she continued the tradition of longevity by serving well over three decades, becoming the only City employee at the old building to maintain employment into the 1990s.

Opposite:

A facelift for the City Hall is applied in February 1940.
The San Jose Mercury News

The duties of these city officials, besides the obvious administrative ones, even included education about city government. In 1942, the *Gilroy Advocate* reported on the annual class visit made by more than twenty Gilroy High School students and their class teacher Olin C. Hadley. They were given a talk by the City Clerk, who "pointed out the workings of the city government and told of city operation under state charters." The students finished the trip with a visit to the jail in the rear of the building; whether or not there were any prisoners in the jail wasn't mentioned.[1] Similarly, Mayor Roberta Hughan recalls that when she was a senior in high school, in 1949-50, she went to the City Hall as part of a day in which students got to sit at someone's desk and learn what was involved in that job. This was part of a government class, and the students could choose whether they wanted to learn about being Mayor or Fire Chief or any other position.[2]

As well as city administration, City Hall was sometimes made available for the use of citizens' organizations. One such instance occurred in 1923, when the City Council voted to make City Hall available as headquarters for the Druids when they held a convention in Gilroy with more than six

hundred delegates. Thus the City Hall was included in what was a big and colorful event, the first time Gilroy hosted a statewide lodge meeting.[3]

The City Hall housed an array of other offices at different times in its history. In late 1940s and early 1950s, the County Health Department office was in the back of the building, upstairs.[4] The Red Cross had a small office upstairs, which was usually staffed by one woman, although volunteers worked there regularly. The Chamber of Commerce occupied an office downstairs at the front of the building, with a window looking out on to Monterey Street. Despite the dispersion of the various offices and functions throughout the building, the people who worked in the City Hall shared a spirit of working together, which easily spilled over into a social camaraderie. This spirit was facilitated by the married couples who worked in the building.

Gilroy Historical Society member Doris Kallas remembers how the building seemed to be the location of life's important passages: she got her first driver's license from Virginia Cox's desk in 1932, and Judge Leon Thomas married her to her husband John in front of the big bay window above

Annual Christmas Tree donated by
Pacific Gas and Electric, 1945.
Courtesy of Mary Prien

tfront door in 1934, the Chaffees, who ran the second hand store next door, standing as their witnesses. In the next few years, she would take her children to the baby clinic upstairs, where Nurse Goodenough introduced her to the principles of health care, under the direction of Dr. Elmer Chesbro. And later in the 1950s, her husband found employment with City Marshal Sturla downstairs, rising through the ranks of the police reserves to become a captain.

The administrative staff of the city soon grew. By the mid-1950s, there were between four and eight people in the City Clerk's office. The expanding staff created a problem of space. In 1958, this problem was solved by the move to the new City Hall facilities at Wheeler Auditorium. For those who had worked in the old building and been irritated by the dust and the plaster created by its age and the constant rumbling of trains going by, or the noise from the traffic on Monterey Street, the move to new facilities was a welcome development. For the Old City Hall, however, the move put its very existence in jeopardy.

Mary Emelia Prien and Eleanor Prien on the steps of City Hall, 1945.
Courtesy of Mary Prien

A face lifting of new stucco was applied in December 1952. The following Spring a new coat of paint revitalized the City Hall. Interior changes included partitioning off part of the court room for a Community Welfare Office and dividing the City Marshal's Office to provide a place to interrogate prisoners.
The San Jose Mercury News

OBVIOUS OBSOLESCENCE: The City Hall Under Threat

The first alarm bell about the fate of the City Hall sounded in 1958 when the City Council finished preparations to move the municipal offices to a wing of the Wheeler Auditorium. This meant that by the middle of that year, the only administrative offices that would be left in the building were the Police Department and the jail. The Chamber of Commerce would still be located there, and the Gilroy Justice Court would stay there temporarily until plans for a new county office building were finalized.

The announcement of these plans immediately raised questions about what was to become of the building in the longer term. City officials received a barrage of questions as to the likely fate of the City Hall. Meanwhile, the City Parking Commission, listing likely sites for parking lots, put the City Hall property at the top of the list and urged that the building be razed as soon as it was vacated.

The *San Jose Mercury* reported on the agitation which spread through Gilroy, in an article titled "Fight On To Save Old Gilroy City Hall."[1] Some Gilroy residents were quite unperturbed about the possible threat to the building. The report noted that one Gilroyan had recently referred to the City Hall disparagingly as a "gingerbread house with gables," and quoted Judge Leon Thomas as saying

that the building had been condemned several years before. It also revealed a general ignorance about the building: "Engineer E.A. Holloway was hired to design the building...but it's not made clear in the records whether he actually was the building's architect. The architectural style is believed to be Flemish, but present City officials are not sure of it."

While the City Hall's popularity was at rock bottom among some circles, there were other Gilroy residents who were fired up to defend it. The article noted that a petition signed by 150 people opposing the destruction of the building had been submitted to the City Council. A resolution also had been received from the Gilroy Grange requesting that the building be preserved as a museum. The Council responded with an assurance that there was no cause for worry, as the police station would be in the City Hall for another two to four years.

Despite the sudden alarm about the issue, fears were indeed premature and soon subsided. The "fight" was not really on until the building was vacated and became truly vulnerable in 1965. In February 1965, the City Council approved the final plans of architect John Hughan for the new Police Administration and Jail Facility.[2] As the building of the new police facility and the evacuation of the Old

City Hall proceeded, the agitation was rekindled.

In December 1965, the City Council received an offer from Walthard Buick who wanted to lease the land at the City Hall site, but the Council rejected the offer because it was "not in a position to lease said land at this time."[3] A few days later the *Gilroy Dispatch* announced that the fateful moment for the Old City Hall had arrived, as the Police Department was to move into its new station at 7370 Rosanna Street the following week.[4] A key document in the decision was the 1963 report made by Consulting Structural Engineer H.J. Brunnier of San Francisco. This structural investigation had resulted in the building being declared "unsafe in the event of a major earthquake." Brunnier, an expert on earthquake safety, declared that the "mortar in the exterior walls is of inferior quality, possessing practically no strength," that "several of the roof trusses have badly split lower chords," that "segmental parapets are particularly hazardous," and generally "that it presents a serious hazard to people in and about it in the event of a major earthquake." His opinion was that any rehabilitation program, "because of the obvious obsolescence of the building, cannot be economically justified."

Fate uncertain in March 1966.
The San Jose Mercury News

GRAVE POSSIBILITIES: To Save Or To Destroy?

The Gilroy City Council revived this report for consideration in January 1966. On January 17th, the Council entered into a contract with Brewster and Greulich, Consulting Structural Engineers of Fresno. For the sum of $1,600, the firm was to produce a report on the costs involved in rehabilitating the Old City Hall. At the same meeting, the Council refused a request from the Civil Air Patrol, Gilroy Squadron No. 24, to rent the building.[1]

At the Council meeting on February 7th, Brewster and Greulich presented and explained their report on the structural condition of the building. The Council ordered the publication of this report and set a public hearing on the disposition of the building for March 7th.[2] The *Gilroy Dispatch* announced that night that "Engineers Say Doom Near For Old City Hall." The article quoted B.J. Greulich as saying that the "building is deficient in all elements.... It would cost in excess of $100,000 to bring it up to modern structural, electrical, plumbing and building codes.... There is a loose keystone in the arch.... The stairways don't meet building code requirements." The next day the *Dispatch* worried that even if the required money was spent, it was "possible that the original character and appearance of the building may be altered due to inability to duplicate the original materials or construction, and it will no longer be the 'city hall' as remembered by many people."[3] More optimistically, the paper concluded that at least "the final choice will be up to the people."

Certainly "the people" had their say at the public hearing on March 7th, having been primed by the publication of both the Brewster and Greulich and the Brunnier reports in full in the *Dispatch* on March 1st. The day after the hearing, the *Dispatch* reported that

speaker after speaker pleaded eloquently to preserve the Monterey St. building.... It became rather apparent from the beginning that the chamber's audience of about 50 were strongly in favor of retaining the old city hall. Most of the speakers cited the historic and sentimental values of the building as well as its unique architectural appearance. The emotion packed audience interrupted several times to boo Councilman Charles Quartiroli who attempted to defend the integrity of the engineers' report.[4]

Particularly noteworthy contributions were made by George Porcella and Margaret Thomas. Porcella said that the main trouble with the old building was neglect and that "As for the 'crack' in the police station archway...he could get an 'old timer' to fix it. It wouldn't take an engineer to repair it. And as for the roof, as far as the eye can see...it is straight as an arrow." Thomas "pointed out the University of California's architectural department has stated that this is the only building left in the state classified as early American with Flemish influence. 'Some years from now, it may be considered as a historic site'."

At the same meeting a letter from Mr. Carl Bolfing was read requesting preservation of the Old City Hall. This letter, both emotive and forthright, described the Old City Hall as representing "the civic pride and sacrifices of the people of Gilroy of 1905; a time when the tax dollar was hard to come by, but the urge for personal sacrifice was strong. I believe they deserve our consideration." Already Bolfing had a clear idea of what the building should become: a museum that will depict "Who, what and why Gilroy is."[5]

After the public hearing closed, the Council decided that the issue of the Hall should be put on the June primary election ballot with a bond issue proposal to raise the money for rehabilitation.[6] However, later in the month, the Council rescinded this decision, preferring "to delay action on the matter until the November 1966 election."[7] The vacillation on the part of the Council was reflected in their instruction to City staff "to investigate other possibilities of aid through other agencies," while the City Engineer was going to talk to Brewster and Greulich about "their philosophy of how they arrived at the estimate on renovation of the Old City Hall." A compromise proposal was elicited from Brewster and Greulich. For $50,000 the building could be preserved as a Historical Museum, which would not conform with the 1961 Uniform Building Code, but would be safe enough for a "historical structure, with mechanical and electrical technology of 1905."[8]

Meanwhile, outside agencies were being drawn into the fray. On April 1st the *Dispatch* announced that the City had received a letter from the Conference of California Historical Societies, headquartered in Stockton, urging preservation of the building. They admonished that "we have received information that there are grave possibilities of your unique and historic City Hall being bulldozed out of existence or so greatly remodeled that it would lose its historical character." The City Council noted this letter at their meeting several days later and were told that George Porcella had contacted the

Opposite:
Standing tall in 1965.
The Gilroy Dispatch

organization for aid in preserving the City Hall.[9] There were further interjections from outside Gilroy during the next few months, including another letter from the Conference of California Historical Societies and letters from the California Pioneers of Santa Clara County and the California Historical Society. All of these letters urged that the City Council should preserve the building because of its historical significance.

BOLFING AT THE HELM: The Gilroy Historical Society Is Formed

On April 1, 1966, the *Dispatch* had briefly mentioned that "a group of historically-conscious Gilroy citizens is working quietly to organize an Historical Society which would make a last ditch fight to keep the Old City Hall." On April 20, it reported that the Society was to hold its first public meeting at 8 p.m. in the City Council Chambers on Friday, April 29, and that Clyde Arbuckle, the San Jose City Historian, was to be the featured speaker. Carl Bolfing, the founder of the new society, announced that at a recent organizational meeting the society had formulated its aims. These included "preservation of the Old City Hall and other landmarks, education in the importance of local history, establishing a museum telling the "story of Gilroy," researching a story of early community builders, and mapping and marking old stage routes and lines of commerce."[1] Besides Carl Bolfing, those who were providing the momentum behind this popular front included George Porcella, Howard Smith, George White, Robert Head, Beth Talcott Fletcher, Margaret Thomas, Kendall Pine, Armand White, Herbert Sheldon and Paul Scheck.

As the forces lined up, the *Gilroy Dispatch* made its allegiance blatantly clear. In an editorial on May 20 it noted that the building "wears an air of

neglect," and besides heartily commending the group of citizens who had formed the Historical Society, it urged "that the Old City Hall be preserved so that it may take its place in our history." On July 13, it protested that a "blanket of silence appears to have fallen over the much discussed and controversial Old City Hall building. No funds have been allocated in the 1966-67 budget for any repair work, and city officials remain mum on the subject." Editorials loudly campaigning on the part of the Historical Society continued to appear on July 15 and July 22.

Al Gagliardi, who was an involved member of the Historical Society, believes that the *Dispatch* played an important role in the crusade. "Once the paper was involved it was a community issue. Editorials tried to sway people too. The paper helped by interviewing people in the street, and found out that their opinion was that the building should be saved, rather than making a parking lot for fifteen cars."[2] He also described the campaign as being "like politics" because it involved talking to people: "conversation was the main thing." The strategy included holding meetings, getting to the City Council to plead the cause, and writing letters to the editor.

In mid-July 1966, the Gilroy Historical Society put a direct proposition to the City Council. Their letter, written by Carl Bolfing, President, was printed in the *Dispatch* on July 13. To begin with they requested the preservation of the Old City Hall. They further suggested that the Council adopt a policy of renovating (minor repairs and painting) and using the building. Specifically, they asked that the Council lease the building to their society for $1.00 per year, for the "sole purpose of the assembling and showing of a museum collection from the local area, and as Headquarters for the Society...to be designated as "The Old City Hall Museum." This letter was presented to the Council at their meeting of July 18th, at which Councilman Goodrich suggested that the City sell the Hall to the Historical Society with an agreement that they renovate it under Council review.[3] The Council agreed to put this to the Society.

This suggestion was received as a move by the Council to abrogate responsibility for the problem. The *Dispatch* editorial on July 22 commented that the suggestion "is no doubt a 'generous' one, but in our opinion is far from sound. The Gilroy Historical Society is a newly formed group...and should not be expected to carry the costly burden of renovating the building." Four days later a lead article quoted Carl Bolfing as saying "It appears to me the council wants to get this thing off their back and we want to preserve it." The article reported on a meeting on July 25th between the Council and the Society, at which it was agreed at least that the first issue to deal with was that of liability insurance covering the building.[4]

Mary Prien, first director of the Gilroy Historical Museum, remembers Carl Bolfing spending many long hours in the City's archives "seeking out all the information that he could, trying to get photos, and finding out who had served there...the City Councilmen, Judges, Mayors, City Clerks and so on. He compiled this and used it in his articles to try to save the building."[5] Bolfing's persistence began to pay off. On July 29, the *Dispatch* ran a lead article with photographs of Mayor Ken Petersen and various members of the Gilroy Historical Society touring the vacant Hall. Bolfing remarked hopefully that "The spirit on both sides is one of cooperation."[6]

The tide began to turn in favor of the Historical Society. City Administrator Wood reported at the August 1st Council meeting that the City's insurance carrier was prepared to give the Historical Society liability insurance at a nominal cost, with the City as co-insured, as long as they agreed that there was to be no "public assemblage" in the building.[7]

Carl Bolfing (known affectionately to many Gilroyans as "Pop" Bolfing) made yet another pitch as reported by the *Dispatch* four days later. "We have something in the Old City Hall that very few

Carl N. "Pop" Bolfing.
The Gilroy Museum

cities in California have," Bolfing proudly asserted. "It points up the civic growth of the community." By now the *Dispatch* was confident enough to state that the City Council "has indicated that it is anxious to accede to the Historical Society's request."[8] Indeed the business was rolling ahead.

At the City Council meeting of September 6, City Administrator Fred O. Wood reported that the City Attorney had prepared a rough draft of an agreement with the Historical Society, based on the outcome of a meeting on August 22nd.

Historical Society members Chuck Gilmore and James Musolino, give a cleaning to the clock faces in 1967.
The Gilroy Museum

PROUD AND CONSCIENTIOUS KEEPERS OF THE BUILDING

On September 19, the City Council hammered out the details of the agreement. Finally on October 24, 1966, the City Council authorized the Mayor Protempore to execute the agreement with the Historical Society.[1] The Historical Society was given a ten-year lease on the building for $1.00 per year, with the conditions that they would not hold public gatherings in it, for insurance reasons, and that they would maintain it and do minor repairs. As part of an interview about the campaign to save the building, in response to the question whether it had been a tough fight, Historical Society member George White calmly replied, "Not too. No, they gave up pretty easy."[2]

The Historical Society had won a well-earned victory. In the same stroke, they had also taken on a serious responsibility. They had no money with which to do the renovations desirable, but they determined to preserve it and keep it clean, as they had promised the City. Al Gagliardi recalls that they painted it, and did a lot of work on the roof, patching it and putting tar on it. Someone would "go there every week, wash the sidewalk and sweep it, and keep the windows clean," and there were regular work parties which would go into the Hall to vacuum and clean, dust and sweep.[3]

In March 1967, there was a "Historical Painting Project," consisting of the donation of a gallon of paint each from members of the Historical Society, and member Tony Silva added a check with his gallon. Another member, Ted Chavez, donated Saturday work on the building with his union crew. This major cosmetic work on the Old City Hall included workers assigned by the City Parks and Recreation Department and paid through the Economic Opportunity Commission. Once the outside was painted, the interior had its turn.[4] A December 1967 account of this work relates that the painters' and plasterers' unions helped out with the painting and plastering involved.[5]

A problem that had plagued the building and its occupants for decades had been the pigeons which loved to congregate there, and the inevitable consequences. This problem had never been solved while the building was in use, despite the never-ending efforts of the police officers to remove pigeon eggs, scare pigeons away, and clean up after them. The Historical Society hit on a solution and installed a few mice and a stuffed owl in the clocktower. For a time it worked beautifully: the pigeons were scared away and found a roost elsewhere, so the job of keeping things clean was much easier.[6] Another

task which the Historical Society assumed was the maintenance of the clock.

The Historical Society did receive some help from the City Council. After receiving a letter from the Historical Society, reporting on their progress with the building, in April 1967 the Council voted to help them out with $1,000 toward renovations.[7] Similarly, in January 1969, the Council approved another $1,000 for the same purpose.[8] In October 1967, the Council also purchased an india ink sketch of the building done by a Mrs. Kaufman,[9] and in November 1967, City workers installed a historic soap kettle from Soap Lake outside the building on the Sixth Street side.[10]

Opposite:

Members of the Gilroy Historical Society gathered on the steps of the Old City Hall building in March 1967 to donate a gallon of paint each toward a new face lifting job. In addition to his gallon of paint, Tony Silva donated a check toward the renovation and is pictured in front, left, handing it to Carl Bolfing, president of the historical society. Behind them from left to right, are: Howard Smith, Irvin Hollister, Ted Chavez, Mayor Ken Petersen, Judge John Klarich, Robert Head, George White and Claude Wright. Chavez donated Saturday work on the building with his union crews.
The Gilroy Museum

The prestige of the building received an important boost from to the Native Daughters of the Golden West in April 1968. The Gilroy Parlor (#312) and the organization's History and Landmarks committee arranged for a bronze plaque to be placed on a cornerstone of the building, dedicated to the memory of pioneers of the area. A Dedication Ceremony was held on April 27, at which the plaque was unveiled, Gilroy school children marched to the site, and the Brownell School Band played the national anthem.[11]

In December 1968, the Gilroy Historical Society made another investment: for $1,200, they purchased the Gilroy Fire Department's old 1923 Seagrave pumper from a Redwood City man and had it returned to Gilroy for display at the Old City Hall.[12] Restoration work on the oak running boards was done by "Pop" Bolfing himself, who took on the Seagrave pumper project as a centerpiece for the Old City Hall Museum which he envisioned. Renovation work also continued. In 1969, new doors were installed in the ground floor to match the original ones. A new roof was put on, windows were fixed, and a brickmason repaired and strengthened parts of the veneer. Workers even discovered the old sloping floors from the building's days as a firehouse.

But the human energy going into the museum, the Seagrave pumper and the Old City Hall itself stopped flowing the day in 1969 when "Pop" Bolfing died at the age of 78.

Gilroy's old city hall stands deserted

By JERRY FUCHS

Once a year Gilroyans can go through the old city hall and gaze in disbelief at the way things used to be. The Historical Society leases the building from the city government for just one dollar a year and has the building stocked with the rarest of things.

Ballusters on winding stairs greet the visitor as he enters the second floor. An American flag with 45 stars is draped over the stairs while the California State Flag is at the top.

Room after room of historical displays and a large hall where at one time the judge held court and the council met before concerned citizens.

The benches in the court are the originals and some are warped, but in otherwise perfect condition. The judge's chair and desk are antique pieces, but would make any office owner proud.

Stairs lead from the second floor to the tower where one of man's first inventions, now run on electric with a crank a day, keeps the time in the old tower going and the bells chiming occasionally.

The old wood ceilings are beautiful and there are few cracks or even pealings showing. A chair here and a chair there, can be spotted to have come from the early 1800s. There are hideaway rooms everywhere once used as offices.

The first floor is not to be missed. The old firehouse and fire engines seen in the Bonanza Days Parade are still on display. Walking past the firehouse one comes into the jail where an old giant vault still adorns a good part of the wall.

There are around six jail cells with stacked cots for the prisoners who were unlucky to make that their destination. From the looks of the jail house portion of the building, this department got a lot of use because here the ceilings are in disrepair.

The old wash basin and switch board that ran on metal plates are still standing. Period costumes from the 1890s and early tools used in Gilroy are on display along with hundreds and hundreds of pictures taken during that period.

And there it all sits, this beautiful, historic building, to be opened to the public just once a year. There are things to be done with that building and old relics to be shared by lovers of antiquity. This building may have its structural flaws, but I would venture to bet it is built more sturdy and safer than the new ones now going up.

What a waste of so much tradition. What a terrible waste of this great location. What are we going to do with the old city hall, continue to open it to the public once a year only during Bonanza Days?

Clerk's desk and records

Judges chambers and council hall

Front Hall with the flag of 1905
containing 45 stars

Mechanism for
the clock and bell

Gilroy's old city hall

THE RAREST OF THINGS: The Museum Within

As the building was being spruced up on the inside and renovated somewhat on the outside, the Historical Society was accumulating artifacts to create the museum which had been dear to its heart during its fight to save the building. When asked from whom they acquired these artifacts, George White commented, "Oh, different people in town. Some we knew, some we didn't know, some came from outside. They just accumulated."[1] Mary Prien recalled that there were original items from the building which were now aptly placed in the museum, such as councilmembers' tables and chairs, and firemen's hats. A *California Historian* article enthusiastically describing the whole renaissance process noted that the acquired artifacts which were going to become part of the museum included an old hose cart from the firehouse, original millstones from the old flour mill in San Ysidro, a large oil painting of one of Henry

Opposite:

The Gilroy Dispatch article about the Historical Society's museum in 1972 may have sparked burglary a week later.
The Gilroy Museum

Miller's horses, and the registration desk from the old Southern Pacific Hotel.[2]

In September, 1972, the *Gilroy Dispatch* ran an article with a very ambivalent message about the museum in the Old City Hall. On one hand, the article described the museum in detail with pride and praise:

The Historical Society has the building stocked with the rarest of things.... The benches in the court are the originals and some are warped, but in otherwise perfect condition. The judge's chair and desk are antique pieces, but would make any office owner proud.... The old wood ceilings are beautiful and here are few cracks or even peelings showing.... The first floor is not to be missed. The old firehouse and fire engines seen in the Bonanza Days parade are still on display.... There are around six jail cells with stacked cots for the prisoners who were unlucky to make that their destination.

On the other hand, however, the paper decried the fact that this experience was only available to the public one day a year during Bonanza Days, while there are "things to be done with that building and old relics to be shared by lovers of antiquity."[3]

The article, published on a Friday and headlined "Gilroy's Old City Hall stands deserted," evidently had an unplanned effect: the building was burglarized that weekend.[4]

Apparently the article did prompt the Historical Society to try to make the displays more available. In 1974, the *Dispatch* ran an article on native Gilroyan Bernice "Babe" Pasley, who volunteered to be in the hall two afternoons a week to tell visitors "tales of the early days."[5]

A NATIONAL HISTORIC PLACE: Renovation, Funding and Leasing

In 1974 the Gilroy City Council decided to nominate the Old City Hall to the National Register of Historic Places (along with the old Episcopal Church), which would also make it eligible for state funding assistance. Gilroy's Parks and Recreation Department, under Director William Ayer, was given the responsibility of applying to the California Department of Parks and Recreation to achieve this. One application was submitted in late 1974, and turned back for revision. The strengthened application, submitted in February 1975, relied on the work of architectural historian David Gebhard in its assertion that the building was designed by Samuel Newsom, the architect of Eureka's Carson House. It noted that the style was either Flemish or Flemish Baroque, although this was a matter of some uncertainty, and stressed the history attached to the building, dedication and uses of the building. The application's main selling point was that "the Old City Hall is a classic example of California Victorian architecture at the turn of the century," and is "one of the only public buildings remaining as an example of Victorian architecture in Central California."[1] This time the application sailed through. The State Historical Resources Commission approved it, sent the nomination on to the National Register office in Washington, where it also passed. On May 10th, 1975, the City was informed that the Old City Hall was now its first building officially listed on the National Register. (In the 1980s, five other Gilroy structures also were added to the Register.)

With this success under its belt, the City turned to the challenge of raising enough money to properly renovate the building. The City officers sweated over what grants were available to the newly-designated landmark, and how the upcoming Bicentennial could be utilized to good effect. Meanwhile, Gilroy's own Bicentennial Committee was energetically organizing functions, the proceeds of which were to go to the renovation of the Old City Hall. Marcel Bracquet, the City's postmaster, was chairman of the committee.

Under the leadership of noted local cultural and historical enthusiast, Howard Smith, the Committee's special efforts were Sunday Tea Dances. Held in the Gilroy Community Center, these dances featured Howard Smith on the piano, and other local talents, swaying the crowd with a host of old-time tunes. The events featured champagne waltz contests, freestyle foxtrot contests, and refreshments.[2] The local community theater also got into the act, donating its profits from a summer production of "1776" to the cause.

The City Council was seriously evaluating what should be done with the Old City Hall. The lease held by the Gilroy Historical Society would soon be running out, and one report quoted city officials as saying that the Society had never even paid its $1.00 per year rent.[3] After some discussion with the Bicentennial Committee, the City applied for a Historic Preservation Grant from the State Parks and Recreation Department, claiming that it would need $100,000 to properly restore the building. The application suggested that, when fully restored, the building could be used for city offices, or a "senior citizens boutique," or meeting space for culturally-oriented community groups.[4]

The City's initiative met with success, although more modest than had been hoped. In March 1976, the State agreed to give $26,000 toward the restoration of the Old City Hall, on condition that the amount be equaled by money raised from local sources.[5] While the Council sought professional opinion on the costs and work involved in the restoration, and some skeptics expressed doubt about the whole enterprise, other energetic Gilroyans continued to raise money. Lola McGahey and Elaine Balke knitted Betsy Ross flags which were displayed in Penney's windows,[6] and the Gilroy Luncheon Optimist Club presented a $500 check toward the cause.[7] City Council opinion on the enterprise was almost evenly divided, but on June 7, 1976, a 4-3 vote went in favor of hiring Frank Laulainen, an architect from Los Gatos, to submit plans for the restoration of the building with a very clear view toward a future commercial use. Laulainen assured the City Council that the building "has great feasibility to be recycled for new use," stressing how it lent "itself romantically and nostalgically to enterprise" and would become a focal point for a commercial revitalization of the downtown area.[8] This was to become an attractive and popular idea for Gilroy's business community.

In July, the City's Parks and Recreation Department requested a second year of grant support from the state Department, estimating that this phase of the restoration would cost $160,000, to be borne by the state and the Gilroy community equally.[9] The disappointment that the grant awarded in January, 1977, was only $14,050, was sharpened by the fact that the architect's estimate for restoration costs was $200,000.[10]

There was, however, a gleam of hope amid all the difficulties. Rumor had broken in November, 1976, that the "famous" Mountain Charley's restaurant in Los Gatos was interested in opening up in the City Hall site. Reporting this rumor, the *Dispatch* whooped "we're on our way!"[11] Plainly campaigning for this project, the *Dispatch* reported on May 4, 1977, that months of talks between the City and the restaurant had borne fruit; two days later it portrayed the negotiation process with a cartoon of Mountain Charley desperately trying to pry open the old stiff door labelled "Old Gilroy City Hall."[12] As if that did not say enough, it claimed "We have eaten at Mountain Charley's in Los Gatos. The food is good, the atmosphere excellent. It...would be a welcome addition to the city."

The Council's next question was whether or not they were prepared to tolerate the word "saloon" as part of the new restaurant's name; while this was being debated, news came that the National Park Service had agreed to give $26,000 toward the restoration, thanks due to Congressman Norm Mineta of San Jose.[13] Everything seemed to be going well: Jim Farwell, president of Mountain Charley Restaurant Corporation, asserted confidently that they would "be grossing more than half a million the first year,"[14] and on August 30, 1977, the *Dispatch* happily announced the signing of the agreement, under which the City would foot the restoration bill and the restaurant was to pay a substantial rent plus 3 1/2% of their gross sales. Even the Gilroy Historical Society was happy with the arrangement; part of the "understanding" with Mountain Charley's was that they would "care for and properly display" many of the "mementoes and artifacts which the society has been able to collect."[15]

Just when the plans seemed to be going smoothly, they fell apart. First there were delays arranging financing for construction. A major problem, however, was the failure by Mountain Charley's to obtain a liquor license, despite earnest attempts. In addition, the principal partners of Mountain Charley's split up, and the designated project manager, Bob Boldazar, succumbed to cancer.[16] The collapse of the plans was announced in the *Dispatch* on June 5, 1978. The City Council did not seem immediately discouraged, however, believing that there were alternatives.

An essential component of the restoration process was carried out in November, 1978, when the entire Old City Hall was wrapped in shrouds by a fumigation company who treated it to rid it of termites.[17] Around the same time, some roof repair work was done. In February, 1979, the City Hall hit the news again: one item was that downtown merchants had as a group asked the City Council to tear down the old Paul's Trading Post next to the Old City Hall on Monterey Street, and to install "wrap-around" parking around Old City Hall, on the basis that this would stimulate downtown commerce.[18] The trading post was later demolished, ironically, by the same crews that were clearing land for the new City Hall building on Rosanna Street. Also in February, there was a promising report that the State Historical Resources Commission, which the previous year had approved a $40,000 grant to be matched by the city for restoration work, and given approval for a plan to

Opposite:

Paul's Trading Post, one of Gilroy's last wood frame business structures, is seen to the left of the City Hall in October, 1977.
The Gilroy Museum

Prepared for fumigation, the City Hall was shrouded in rubberized nylon tarp in November 1978.
The Gilroy Dispatch

put in reinforced concrete pilasters to support the walls.[19]

Other matters were moving along also: City Administrator Fred O. Wood sent out a request for proposals for a "food service establishment" on a lease basis in the Old City Hall. In May, 1979, the City Council resolved to apply for federal funds from the grants program administered by the State Office of Historic Preservation.[20] At the City Council meeting on Monday, June 4, 1979, a brand new possibility was presented: Hoffman and Associates of Watsonville proposed that they would purchase the City Hall for $200,000 and the land around it for $100,000 over a ten year period, and would pay 2/3 of the restoration costs if the city would come up with the other third.

The principals, Jeff and Roger Hoffman, informed the Council frankly that the proposal from their point of view was not to make a profit, but rather to provide a tax shelter for investors. The Council was unanimous in its lack of enthusiasm for the deal, saying that it was a bad deal for the city. Some council members clearly opposed the idea of selling the building.[21] Pushing ahead, the council formed a three-member subcommittee (consisting of Jack Pate, Roberta Hughan and David Stout) to deal with the question of the building's fate.

On June 11, 1979, reporting that the newly-formed subcommittee had recommended that the Old City Hall be leased rather than sold, the *Gilroy Dispatch* supported this view in its editorial: "We agree that Gilroy's Old City Hall should remain in public ownership to guarantee its preservation. Once ownership is out of the city's hands it would be difficult to control the destiny of the historical landmark." Meanwhile, the Monterey Street frontage of the building was rented to the South Santa Clara County Housing Development Corporation, while the rest of the building stored dusty exhibits from the Bicentennial.

In August 1979, the City Council ran a public notice that until October 1st they would be accepting proposals to lease the Old City Hall. In late October, it was reported that the Old City Hall subcommittee had met with Hoffman and Associates again, this time to discuss their proposal to rehabilitate and rent the building rather than buy it.[22] Around the same time, the Santa Clara County Board of Supervisors adopted a county heritage inventory, which included the Old City Hall.[23]

MONTEREY STREET MELT: The Old City Hall Restaurant

On January 21, 1980, the Gilroy City Council approved an agreement with Hoffman and Associates of Watsonville to lease them the Old City Hall. The agreement included the specification that the lessees would contribute $494,110 toward restoration costs, while the city itself would put up $100,000. In consideration of this, there was to be only $1 per year in rent charged for the first ten years, after which the Hoffmans would pay an annual rent of $25,000 which would increase after five years.[1]

On Wednesday, January 23, the *Dispatch* reported that the Historical Society had proudly announced that it had set aside approximately $10,000 in a high interest account for "frosting on the cake" after the restoration was complete.[2] This was the grand sum that had been raised by the Bicentennial Committee's efforts such as the tea dances and other fund raisers. This money was later transferred to a City account.

Restoration work began, but it was a slow and painful process. By December, 1980, most of the work had been done on the outside of the building, including painting, roof repairs, re-setting of windows, and the restoration of the clock to its old pendulum works. However, Jeff Hoffman reported that the fluctuations in the economy had put interest rates beyond what his company could afford, and that they would have to wait for interest rates to fall before they could proceed with work on the interior.[3] At first, Hoffman and Associates had thought they might put boutiques and specialty shops in the building, but by mid-1981 a marketing study had persuaded them that a restaurant was the best venture. To placate the City Council about the delay, and to show them what they might expect, Hoffman invited three Council members over to their successful Mansion House restaurant in Watsonville for lunch.[4]

For more than a year little happened. Then on September 17, 1982, Hoffman invited Gilroy's Chamber of Commerce to an evening in the Old City Hall in order to inform them of the restoration progress and the restaurant plans.[5] Hoffman proudly announced that finance for the project was now arranged, and that construction was to begin in early December. Architecturally, the building was to be kept intact, except for a hole torn in the court-room floor to install a new circular glass stairway. This was done "to give the diners the feeling they are all sharing the same space."[6] Also, a 1,500 square foot addition was made in the back to house the

Historical photos and comfortable dining.
Courtesy of the City of Gilroy

The new glass stairway became controversial for
many Gilroyans. *Courtesy of the City of Gilroy*

Opposite: Workers paint the City Hall in preparation for its new life. *The San Jose Mercury News*

kitchen, and a courtyard was designed to fill the vacant lot adjacent to the building on its northern side.[7]

In January 1983, Hoffman optimistically announced that the restaurant would be open by summer to "catch the summer market."[8] But in September, it was announced that the opening would be delayed until mid-December.[9] Finally, the $1.5 million restoration and refurbishing job was complete. On December 27, the *Dispatch* bally-hooed the event: "People tonight will be cracking open lobster tails and dipping spoons into gooey desserts where once city fathers deliberated zoning issues. Dancers will glide to piano music where a judge once dispensed justice."[10] The event was a gala opening with two hundred guests, including city officials and business leaders. The restaurant was open to the public for dinner a few days later and opened for the lunch crowd in January. The interior design of the restaurant was hailed as startling, with its art deco style, salmon and black color scheme and high-gloss bar.

Mayor Roberta Hughan was enthusiastic about the success of the Hoffman enterprise: she felt that they restored the building in a way that kept the historical flavor, that the decor was good, and the whole "delightful."[11] Some others, however, were dismayed that the floor of the courtroom had been removed. They felt that with the courtroom gone, much of the historical integrity of the building had been lost. Al Gagliardi, a member of the City's Historical Heritage Committee, felt that the Committee should have had input over the interior as well as exterior modifications. He believed that opposition to removing the floor was ignored.[12]

Hoffman and Associates, naturally, were pleased and enthusiastic about their new business. Speaking of the interior design, Jeff Hoffman said "We tried to write history through architecture and design." They believed that authentic historic restoration required that it should be clear to people

The historic stairway still led one to the refurbished clock high above. *Courtesy of the City of Gilroy*

Art deco style marked the new bar. On the left reinforced concrete pillars framed the glass entryway to the patio built where Paul's Trading Post once stood. *Courtesy of Chuck Myer*

what is original and what isn't. For that reason they preserved historic interior elements such as the judge's railing and the original wooden banisters and trim, and left those elements to co-exist with the new art deco interior work. The restaurant featured an outdoor patio, a split-level dining area where the firehouse had once been, and incorporated small plaques at various points which explained what the functions of each room, such as the justice court, assembly hall, and council chambers, had been.[13] One of the more intriguing features of the 350-seat restaurant was that the bathrooms were located in the old jail cells, preserved for posterity.

Hoffman was confident that the restaurant would succeed: "the quality of the food and service is going to make this a first-class operation that the community will support." In June 1984, it seemed successful when a local newspaper columnist said that the restaurant "has certainly carved out its niche in the upper echelons of the South County's restaurants. Its surprisingly modern interior decor provides a very pleasant dining atmosphere."[14]

In April 1985, the Old City Hall Restaurant announced that its courtyard was open, that they were serving cioppino feeds on Friday evenings, and the Sunday Swing Club served up live jazz on Sunday evenings.[15] A ceremony was held in the courtyard that month to dedicate a plaque to the memory of Carl "Pop" Bolfing, who had put so much individual effort into forming the Gilroy Historical Society and saving the Old City Hall from destruction.

These good spirits, however, were short-lived. In June, restaurant manager Beverly Owens announced that the restaurant would no longer be open for lunch, because they were not doing enough noontime business to maintain profit above the overhead. She said they would, nevertheless, still be open for dinner and Sunday brunch.[16] But a month later, Hoffman and Associates announced that the restaurant was closed and the business was up for sale. They blamed the failure on poor management.[17] Gilroy residents attributed the failure of the venture to various causes: high prices of the meals, the poor service, the distance from the tables to the kitchen, and the fact that the Harvest Time Restaurant across the street at the old Milias Hotel was stiff competition.

In one day, the restaurant was abandoned: opened liquor bottles remained at the bar, food was left out in the kitchen, and place settings remained at the tables for months afterwards. Tales of employee infighting and restaurant mismanagement cropped up during the next year. The vandalized premises were left to vagrants, and stray cats stalked the scores of pigeons that had returned to nest in the belfry. Valuable artwork was stolen from the deserted banquet halls, the intricate place settings became engulfed in cobwebs, and the pendulum in the clock tower wound down and came to a standstill.

II. "The Old Lady Is Fine": A New Lease On Life

by Chuck Myer

FROSTING ON THE CAKE: The Old City Hall Committee

Throughout 1985 the building's fate lay shrouded in private business dealings. The City government watched helplessly, denied even access to the building, as the Hoffman brothers attempted to escape their losses through resales, transfers and finally bankruptcy proceedings. A year earlier, Mayor Roberta Hughan had appointed an Old City Hall Committee to oversee the preservation of the historic status of the Old City Hall and to disburse funds which were collected as part of the Bicentennial project to save the structure and later dedicated to "frosting on the cake" by the Gilroy Historical Society. The committee included 1976 chairman Marcel Bracquet and City Historian Howard Smith, as well as Councilwoman Sharon Albert. The new committee was chaired by a historian, Dr. James Williams of Gavilan College, and it now became the City's focal point in keeping a hand in the historical preservation of the building.

A dedication ceremony held on April 27, 1985 was one of the committee's first official actions. Following the City's annual Cultural Arts Faire on Fifth Street, a parade with an honor guard and Dixieland music processed down Monterey Street to Sixth Street. In the recently completed courtyard (the former site of Paul's Trading Post), a plaque and portrait of Carl "Pop" Bolfing were dedicated and hung as a reminder of his lifetime efforts to save the building from demolition. In attendance were many of Bolfing's descendants, including the late Byron Bolfing, brother of Carl, who revealed at the unveiling of the portrait that he was the photographer. The committee also displayed and dedicated the 1776 Bennington flag it had purchased for the flagstaff above the building's clocktower to commemorate the Bicentennial Committee's efforts.[1]

Meanwhile, the committee also authorized

Al Gagliardi pays tribute to "Pop" Bolfing as Chuck Myer looks on.
Photos Courtesy of Chuck Myer

Opposite:

Bill Kuring's antique Cadillac leads the dedication ceremony procession down Fifth Street to the Old City Hall.

Byron Bolfing (left) and Chuck Gilmore, "Pop" Bolfing's brother and grandson, unveil the photograph and plaque in the Old City Hall courtyard, April 27, 1985.

preparation of a preservation maintenance schedule for the building and retained utility crews to remove the power pole in front of the building on the Sixth Street side which obstructed views and had long been the bane of local photographers. In August, all of the nearby poles and wires were placed underground allowing a clear, unobstructed view of the City Hall's facade. They also began doing research towards their next goal: the preparation of a book about the Old City Hall. Based on the recommendation of Chairman Jim Williams, the Old City Hall Committee commissioned a U.C. Santa Barbara professor and his research assistant, Carroll Pursell and Angela Woollacott, to research and document the colorful history of the Old City Hall.[2]

Shortly thereafter, hard times fell on the restaurant's management, and the business closed in mid-1985. Hoffmann and Associates claimed to have sold their 49-year lease ($1-a-year for the first ten years) to Joel Vicars III of Arlington, Virginia.[3] The Old City Hall Committee, like most local residents, felt dispossessed of their treasured landmark.

An ironic turn of events followed. The Committee's city staff liaison, Chuck Myer, attempted to contact of the investor/ leaseholder in order to obtain entrance to the closed facility. It was only then that the City of Gilroy learned to its amazement that no private entity but the federal government actually controlled the building. The

Hoffmans had evidently defaulted on a loan from the Small Business Administration and later declared bankruptcy. To the City's further dismay, it also was learned that the SBA intended to recoup its loss through the sale of all of the building's contents, and that an auction date had already been set! Auctioneer Millard Dove, a fan of historic structures himself, had begun a careful inventory of the contents and had even prepared a glossy photo brochure of the items to be auctioned.

Acting quickly, City Administrator Jay Baksa and the Gilroy City Council made an offer on the entire package: the business, the building's contents (including kitchen supplies, silverware, booths, etc.). As an added bonus, the City requested that the previous $1-a-year lease be also included in the bill of sale. Dove accepted the City's offer of $101,650, and closed the deal on behalf of the SBA before the auction ever took place. Suddenly, the City of Gilroy was in the restaurant business and, more importantly, was back in control of its most important cultural resource. The building and its refurbishments were in local hands and could again be leased, this time with terms much more favorable to the City of Gilroy and its taxpayers.

The building, vacant for a year, was again in need of repair. The City did its own inventory and recorded the missing items, including mounted posters of historic photographs and a commissioned mural, designed by Helen Webber, based on local

The abandoned Old City Hall Restaurant Kitchen.
Courtesy of the City of Gilroy

photographs by John A. White, Jr. City crews and volunteers continued to clean and restore the premises. Fake owls were used again to scare away pigeons, while the combined efforts of Gene Corriden, Ralph Blackburn and Chuck Myer were able to bring the historic clock back to working and running order.

In addition, the committee was successful in obtaining a $27,000 grant from the State Office of Historic Preservation for additional structural work, seismic safety, clock repairs, and "building stabilization" (care and treatment and repointing of historic masonry surfaces). A summary of the building's appearance was presented in the grant application:

At the time of its construction in 1905, Gilroy's Old City Hall was described as "begabled, beportholed and beturreted," and so it exists to this day. Although the builder described it as being "in the mission style," its ornate and complex design can best be described as Flemish Baroque, due to the use of whimsically curved lines and a multiplicity of functionless decoration.

The sandstone block first story gives the building its solidness, and surrounds the various arched doors and windows, hooded with fancy curved gables, including the large platform front stairway, which leads to the big double door front entrance. The second story, brick and stucco over wood framing, consists of a series of round and arched windows, outlined in sandstone blocks, and often hooded with oversized bracketed gables. The most imposing and spectacular feature is the bell tower and clock which rises from the top of the second floor, topped with an appropriate finial. The four faces of the large clock are visible for several blocks.

The tower and roof are covered with tile.

The exterior of the structure remains basically the same in appearance at it did in 1906, with a few exceptions. Rehabilitation of the structure in 1981-83 converted it for historic reuse as a restaurant. The arched doorways of the old fire department which crown the southern facade, were retained and highlighted with a lighted atrium effect. A new kitchen building was added adjacent to the historic structure, and a landscaped courtyard was added along the northern facade. Paint and trim detailing have been faithful to the original appearance. The interior of the building was done in a modern decor to clearly differentiate the original from the new.[1]

Many assumed that seismic safety had been assured by the restoration work done by the Hoffmans. But the foreboding cracks in the restaurant lobby after the 1984 Morgan Hill earthquake made it clear that the building was still susceptible to the earth's motions. The grant proposal was strengthened in that area, and resubmitted to the State.

The search began for a business enterprise which would restore the restaurant in either a similar or modified format. Other uses were considered, as well as multi-use arrangements with the Gilroy Museum or the Library and Culture Commission. One ambitious but ill-fated plan, put forward by Dick Smithee, called for a community-operated facility with front money from the City and profits earmarked for preserving the historic Strand Theater downtown.[5] The civic nature of the Smithee proposal prompted another interested group of investors, led by Ed Lazzarini, to step aside temporarily so as not to be perceived as being anti-community.

In December 1986, the Old City Hall was reopened to the public for a downtown revitalization event. The central glass staircase, added by the Hoffmans, became a podium from which both floors could be addressed. It turned out to be the last time the staircase would be used.

THE FRED AND ED SPECIAL: The Restaurant Changes Flavors

In mid-1987, negotiations were completed with Ed Lazzarini and Fred Lombardi to reopen the restaurant after the Smithee proposal was retracted. Modifications were made to the interior which actually returned the building much closer to its original two-floor design. The circular glass stairway was removed, and a hardwood floor was placed upstairs for dancing. A huge garlic-shaped chandelier installed by the Hoffmans was modified to fit the restaurant's new design. The railing in the old courtroom was not moved, while the new owners did more than $100,000 worth of renovation work. The concept for the new restaurant was an emphasis on "Early Californian" cuisine; in fact, the proposed name for the business was "Eduardo's Cantina." The owners later decided to retain the name "Old City Hall."

The restaurant's grand reopening dazzled diners on September 9, 1987. Shortly thereafter, the lower dining hall was dedicated to "Pop" Bolfing, and his portrait was rehung in a prominent place. Menu selections now included items like seafood and pasta dishes, and "The Fred and Ed Special." In January 1988, the rejuvenated banquet facility was used to host four visitors from the Soviet Union. The gala event pulled in local civic and media personalities, and reintroduced the community to the historic space which had served as the courthouse and council chambers for so many years. Other civic events followed in the new upstairs facility.

In April 1989, South Valley Civic Theatre produced a Neil Simon comedy, "Chapter Two," in the upstairs courtroom. This event proved to be the precursor of coming events: owners Lazzarini and Lombardi were taken with the potential of performing live theatre in the old courtroom. They began negotiations with local theater entrepeneurs Russ and Nancy Hendrickson of "Center Stage," whose outgrown facility was located about a block away. The Hendricksons, too, saw the potential for live theater downtown. Together, they discussed the possibility of not only moving their theater to the Old City Hall, but managing the restaurant business as well. The Hendricksons felt strong familial ties to the historic old building. Through Nancy's family tree, the Gilmores, Bolfings and Forsyths, they had long been associated with the Old City Hall. Carl "Pop" Bolfing was Nancy's grandfather.

Lazzarini and Lombardi developed a plan for a smooth transition period, after which the

Hendricksons would control the operation of the business, with "Fred and Ed" as silent partners. The new scheme would center around the "Old City Hall Restaurant and Playhouse," which would blend entertainment with dining on a scale not previously attempted in Gilroy. Brunch performances, multi-level cabaret seating, tour shows, outdoor jazz, original productions and even singing waiters were all in the plans.[1] The chance that Gilroy's historic Monterey Street might again host theatrical productions appealed to downtown business owners and old-timers who remembered the glory days of the Strand Theater a block-and-a-half to the north. (Efforts to preserve the Strand failed in 1988 when the theater was converted to accommodate expansion of a retail store.)

On June 30, 1989, the first Hendrickson production opened in the Old City Hall as a private benefit for the Philanthropic Educational Organization. On July 17, 1989, the Council approved the transfer of the lease to the Hendricksons. That same month a comedy, "Let's Murder Marsha," starring Rod, Marion and Whitney Pintello, became the first Center Stage production to be held in the "Old City Hall Playhouse." Slowly the Hendricksons moved to build their vision. A Saturday night in

Advertisement in *The Gilroy Dispatch*, November 1987.

August, 1989, featured an event they hoped would become a regular one: a murder-mystery banquet, at which one of the diners is "murdered" (between courses!) and the others are left to interpret clues towards solving the "heinous crime." Billed as "a Silver Screen Affair," the event utilized the early Hollywood motif they hoped to incorporate into the permanent decor.

Unwanted controversies sprung up during the Fall of 1989. The poor condition of the well-worn Bennington flag was noted by the *San Jose Mercury News.*[2] Strings of old Christmas lights hampered access to the flagpole on the treacherous belltower; the flag was finally removed. Also, state historians balked at the removal of the railing along the judge's bench, necessitated by theatrical requirements; a pledge was made to preserve it elsewhere. The question of access for the handicapped also became a community-wide issue. Since the Hendrickson's proposal called for special activities upstairs, wheelchair-bound customers had only the historic stairways to get them to the main stage. Knowing that the construction of an elevator would impact the historic fabric of the building, City staffers, contractors, citizens, and representatives of the handicapped community struggled together with the Hendricksons toward a solution.

The events of October 17, 1989, served to make these issues moot.

THE QUAKE OF 1989: History Repeats Itself

On the afternoon of Tuesday, October 17, 1989, Russ Hendrickson made the rounds, wearing the suspenders and tie he hoped to make his trademark as the entrepreneur/maitre de of the Old City Hall Restaurant and Playhouse. He strolled by the attractive bar, chatting with the after lunch crowd. Leisurely enjoying the unseasonably good weather in the covered courtyard, they were charmed by his stories of early Hollywood days. As the afternoon wore, anticipation began to build for the World Series game that was to start around 5:30 p.m. The bar buzzed with bets and blarney. As the early dinner guests started arriving after work, the evening's specials were scrawled on the backlit, colored chalkboard. Suddenly dishes were rattling, glasses were breaking, hearts were pounding.

A 7.1 earthquake rumbled through Northern California, causing havoc and heartbreak far and near.

Opposite:

Two weeks after the Loma Prieta Quake, Steve Garcia and other construction workers begin to shore up "The Old Lady".
The San Jose Mercury News

Reactions were mixed; though there didn't seem to be serious damage to the building, plaster and paint were cracked and crumbling in several locations, particularly inside the front facade. Some diners still planned to dine, and Russ was ready to serve them. Yet some employees were a little shaken: What if it was just a foreshock? What happened at my house? Soon it was clear that things were not going to go on as usual, the way they usually did after any other California jolt. Across the street, the unreinforced brick wall at Hall's Clothing Store fell through the roof of the store next door. Cracks loomed large in store fronts up and down Monterey. The Old City Hall, though still standing, was shaken. Badly shaken.

That evening, building inspectors made it official: the restaurant was shut down indefinitely. Closer inspections revealed that the already weakened mortar was virtually useless in masonry walls in the front and rear. The bricks were standing together due to the sheer inertia of their own weight. Nothing was holding the huge curved glass window to its moorings directly above the front door. One tap sent it sailing to the steps below, shattering an irreplaceable relic into worthless shards.

City crews began removing loose bricks before an

A year later, the Old City Hall awaits funding for rehabilitation, held up by some $40,000 worth of timber. *The San Jose Mercury News*

aftershock, or even the wind, could do it for them. The mortar was so poor that the yellow ornamental bricks below the clock and standard red bricks above the old jail could be removed effortlessly by hand. Plastic was spread to cover the gaping holes and protect the interior from rain. On the front door, the Hendricksons had scrawled an optimistic slogan for their worried patrons: "The Old Lady is Fine."

As the days went by, more problems were uncovered. A local contracting firm, Farotte Construction, was hired to brace the most insecure sections of the structure. Floor tiles and boards were removed to make way for huge timbers to support the topheavy clocktower and front facade. Structural engineers in hard hats examined the building, shaking their heads as the estimates multiplied: $200,000 -- $400,000 -- three-quarters of a million -- one and a quarter million. More than any other structure in Gilroy, the Old Lady had taken the brunt of nature's pounding; the four clock faces, which had been right on time, said 5:04 p.m.

Gilroy soon realized that history seemed to be repeating itself. "Newspaper and oral records of the 1906 earthquake," reported the *Dispatch* in November, are almost eerily similar to accounts of last month's quake."[1] As in 1906, communities around Gilroy fared much worse. Ironically, both Mountain Charley's in Los Gatos and the Mansion House in Watsonville were ravaged even more by the quake than Gilroy's downtown, which escaped fairly well intact. The realization that the Old City Hall had endured both of the century's worst earthquakes, 83 years apart, endeared even more citizens to its "beportholed" gables. The state's finest historic preservationists and structural engineers were consulted to help save and rebuild her one more time, to preserve her for one more generation.

San Jose Mercury News architecture critic Alan Hess summed up best the importance of Gilroy's Old City Hall in the 1990s:

The best South Bay city halls were all built around the turn of the century--every last one now bulldozed except for a little gem in Gilroy.

The Garlic Capital's former city hall is recognized as a superb example of place-making. In this small town it stands out. It's clearly not a commercial building. It's clearly not a church. It's clearly not a school. It's a building for all the citizens.

Its wide corner steps lead up to a grand staircase shoehorned into a space the size of a telephone booth. Its fanciful tower and gables are a carefree rendition of the mission style, a bit more Dutch than they are supposed to be. The pride of the small town shows through. The Newsoms packed a lot of civic pride into a small container....

Architects [of today's new city halls] should remember the simple lessons of Gilroy's Old City Hall.[2]

III. Not Another One Like It Anywhere: The Building's Significance

Gilroy's Old City Hall is architecturally unique, a building to be appreciated and preserved for its physical merits alone. More than that, it also bears all the significance which Gilroy's citizens have attached to it over the years: it embodies more of Gilroy's history than any other building. The *Gilroy Dispatch* stated unequivocally in an editorial in May, 1966: "Not only is the Old City Hall a landmark, it gives our town an identity, an identity which cannot be replaced. In a day of look-alike conformity, we feel that our city officials should make every effort to preserve the building."[1]

The best measure of the City Hall's significance are the testimonies of longtime Gilroy residents. Mary Prien says that she's for preserving the building because it has always been impressive to her: "it's home...part of the community...the one

building that has always been there."[2] Frances Howson Vigna says that she "grew up fond of that building and would scream if anyone talked of demolishing it, because it is unique, there's not another one like it anywhere. That building is Gilroy, and I'm very loyal to Gilroy. And I'm very loyal to that old building."[3] Al Gagliardi recalls that when the building was under threat in the mid-1960s "there was a pretty strong hue and cry to save that building.... It meant a lot to a lot of people."[4] Mayor Roberta Hughan's view is that the "building is very important.... It was a true landmark for the community.... Architecturally it's very consistent. It's a well-designed building in the sense that it all fits together."[5]

When in 1904 Mayor Dunlap and the Gilroy City Council planned to build a new city hall, they had a vision of a building that would by its sheer grandiosity convey an image of Gilroy as a thriving, burgeoning community. Gilroy's Old City Hall embodies their hopes, memories of California travellers over decades, much of Gilroy's history, and an abundance of associations for Gilroy's residents.

Angela Woollacott and Carroll Pursell

Opposite:

Looking West along Fifth Street gives a new perspective to The Old City Hall. October 1977. *The Gilroy Museum*

DOCUMENTATION

FOR FURTHER READING

The information from which this book was written came from four major sources: the Minutes of the Gilroy City Council, the files of the city's several newspapers, newspaper clippings concerning the City Hall and its restoration kept by the City Planning Department, and oral interviews with citizens who were kind enough to share their recollections of the town and building.

A small published literature exists on the history of Gilroy itself. Of particular interest are a collection of essays edited by James C. Williams, *Sketches of Gilroy* (Gilroy, 1980) published by the Gilroy Historical Society, *Pieces of the Past: A Story of Gilroy* by Claudia Kendall Salewske (Gilroy, 1982), and *Gilroy's First Century of Incorporation, 1870-1970: A History of the City* (Gilroy, 1970).

Opposite:

In June, 1985, Joel Goldsmith, Debra Tibbs, and Bill Ayer deliver flowers donated by Goldsmith Seeds for planting along Monterey Street by Volunteers. *The San Jose Mercury News*

ENDNOTES

I. REFLECTING CREDIT UPON OUR PEOPLE: Gilroy's Old City Hall

A STONE EDIFICE: Building City Hall

1. See Tim Hogan, "Pleasant Valley Promotion: The Story of Gilroy Boosterism, 1868-1907," in James C. Williams, ed., *Sketches of Gilroy*, California (Gilroy, 1980), pp. 29-35.
2. *Gilroy Advocate*, February 27, 1904.
3. *Souvenir Magazine of Gilroy, Santa Clara County, California* (San Jose, c. 1905).
4. *Gilroy Advocate*, April 9, 1904.
5. *Gilroy Advocate*, April 9, 1904.
6. *Souvenir Magazine of Gilroy.*
7. *Gilroy Advocate*, May 7, 1904.
8. *Gilroy Advocate*, June 11, 1904.
9. Gilroy City Council, Minutes, August 1, 1904.
10. *Ibid.*
11. *Gilroy Advocate*, August 6, 1904.
12. *Gilroy Advocate*, September 24, 1904.
13. *Gilroy Advocate*, August 6, 1904.
14. *Gilroy Advocate*, September 3, 1904.
15. Gilroy City Council, Minutes, September 6,

1904; *Gilroy Advocate,* September 10, 1904.

16. Gilroy City Council, Minutes, September 28, 1904 and October 4, 1904; *Gilroy Advocate,* October 8, 1904.

17. Wolfe died in 1926. See his obituary in *The Architect and Engineer,* 86 (September, 1926), 114.

18. For example, see Gilroy City Council, Minutes, October 11, 1904.

19. Gilroy City Council, Minutes, October 27, 1904 and November 7, 1904.

20. Gilroy City Council, Minutes, November 12, 1904, November 14, 1904, November 26, 1904, and December 20, 1904.

21. Gilroy City Council, Minutes, November 14, 1904 and November 26, 1904.

22. Gilroy City Council, Minutes, January 3, 1905.

23. *Gilroy Gazette,* April 14, 1905.

24. *Gilroy Gazette,* May 12, 1905.

25. Gilroy City Council, Minutes, May 29, 1905.

26. Gilroy City Council, Minutes, June 19, 1905, July 3, 1905 and August 10, 1905.

27. *Gilroy Gazette,* September 1, 1905.

28. Gilroy City Council, Minutes, August 25, 1905, September 11, 1905, September 25, 1905 and October 2, 1905.

29. Claudia Kendall Salewske, *Pieces of the Past: A Story of Gilroy* (Rev. ed., Gilroy, 1982), pp. 66, 20; *Gilroy Advocate,* January 21, 1943.

30. *Gilroy Gazette,* November 3, 1905.

31. City Council of Gilroy, Minutes, November 6, 1905, December 18, 1905 and December 12, 1905.

WE WILL REMEMBER MONDAY: Cornerstone and Dedication

1. *Gilroy Gazette,* "Extra," November 22, 1905.
2. *Gilroy Gazette,* January 19, 1906.

AWFUL CATASTROPHE: The quake of 1906

1. *Gilroy Advocate,* April 21, 1906 and *Gilroy Gazette,* April 20, 1906.

2. Gilroy City Council, Minutes, April 23, 1906, May 8, 1906 and May 10, 1906; *Gilroy Gazette,* May 18, 1906.

3. Gilroy City Council, Minutes, June 18, 1906 and July 12, 1906; *Gilroy Gazette,* June 29, 1906 and July 20, 1906.

4. Gilroy City Council, Minutes, September 14, 1906.

5. *Gilroy Advocate,* September 15, 1906.

6. *Gilroy Advocate,* September 22, 1906; *Gilroy Gazette,* Sept. 28, 1906.

7. *Gilroy Advocate,* October 6, 1906.

8. *Gilroy Advocate,* December 8, 1906; Gilroy City Council, Minutes, December 17, 1906.

9. *Gilroy Advocate,* July 13, 1907.

10. *Gilroy Gazette,* February 2, 1907.

11. Gilroy City Council, Minutes, July 16, 1907, July 24, 1907, August 12, 1907 and January 14, 1908.
12. Gilroy City Council, Minutes, August 5, 1907; *Gilroy Advocate,* August 10, 1907.
13. Gilroy City Council, Minutes, October 7, 1907.

FOR THE RECEPTION OF BOOKS: The Library

1. Gilroy City Council, Minutes, November 6, 1905.
2. Gilroy City Council, Minutes, December 12, 1905 and January 2, 1906.
3. Gilroy City Council, Minutes, February 5, 1906; *Gilroy Advocate,* February 2, 1907.
4. Gilroy City Council, Minutes, August 5, 1907.
5. Gilroy City Council, Minutes, December 7, 1908.

MARVELOUSLY BAROQUE: Architect and Style

1. David Gebhard et al., *A Guide to Architecture in San Francisco and Northern California* (Santa Barbara, 1973), p. 183.
2. David Gebhard et al., *Samuel and Joseph Cather Newsom: Victorian Architectural Imagery in California, 1878-1908* (Santa Barbara, 1979), p. 31.
3. Phyllis Filiberti Butler, *The Valley of Santa Clara: Historic Buildings, 1792-1920* (San Jose, 1975), p. 186; Gebhard et al., *A Guide to Architecture* p. 444.
4. *San Jose Mercury,* November 7, 1965.

PROCLAIMING THE FLIGHT OF TIME: The Tower Clock and Bell

1. Gilroy City Council, Minutes, March 12, 1906; Claudia Kendall Salewske, *Pieces of the Past: A Story of Gilroy,* 1982), p. 66.
2. Gilroy City Council, Minutes, December 1, 1913; *Gilroy Advocate,* December 6, 1913. The clock has a nameplate on its cast iron base, inscribed "Seth Thomas Clock Co., Thomaston, Conn., USA, Dec. 31, 1913, No. 1859."
3. *Gilroy Advocate,* February 7, 1914.
4. Gilroy City Council, Minutes, March 2, 1914.
5. Interview, May 23, 1986.
6. Myer, Chuck, "As Time Goes By: The Story of Gilroy's Old City Hall Clock," for California Pioneers of Santa Clara County, 1987.
7. Interview with Nancy McCarthy, *Gilroy Dispatch,* March, 1987.
8. Interview with Mrs. Elizabeth and Mr. Philip Lawton, July 7, 1986.
9. Interview with Charles Gilmore, Sr., March 19, 1990.
10. *Gilroy Dispatch,* September 28, 1982.
11. Interview, May 23, 1986.
12. Interview, May 23, 1986.

THOUSANDS WILL PASS THROUGH OUR CITY:
Improving Monterey Street

1. Gilroy City Council, Minutes, June 7, 1912.
2. Gilroy City Council, Minutes, April 7, 1913.
3. Gilroy City Council, Minutes, May 31, 1913.
4. *Gilroy Advocate*, May 16, 1914.
5. Gilroy City Council, Minutes, August 26, 1913 and March 5, 1917.

HEATED RIVALRY: The Volunteer Fire Companies

1. Gilroy City Council, Minutes, October 3, 1904.
2. Vigilant Engine Co. No. 1, Minutes, September 7, 1904.
3. Vigilant Engine Co. No. 1, Minutes, October 3, 1906.
4. Eureka Hook and Ladder Co., No. 1, Minutes, February 4, 1907 and March 7, 1907; Gilroy City Council, Minutes, February 4, 1907.
5. Vigilant Engine Co. No. 1, Minutes, May 6, 1908; Eureka Hook and Ladder Co. No. 1, Minutes, September 3, 1908, October 1, 1908, February 4, 1909, May 6, 1909 and November 4, 1909.
6. Gilroy City Council, Minutes, January 12, 1909, January 4, 1910 and March 7, 1910; Eureka Hook & Ladder Co. No. 1, Minutes, January 6, 1910.

7. Gilroy City Council, Minutes, March 6, 1911; Eureka Hook and Ladder Co. No. 1, Minutes, April 5, 1911, December 4, 1913 and July 2, 1914.
8. *Gilroy Advocate*, March 25, 1916.
9. Gilroy City Council, Minutes, February 24, 1916.
10. *Gilroy Advocate*, February 26, 1916.
11. Gilroy City Council, Minutes, March 20, 1916, March 22, 1916 and April 11, 1916.
12. Eureka Hook and Ladder Co. No. 1, Minutes, September 6, 1916; Vigilant Engine Co. No. 1, Minutes, September 6, 1916.
13. Eureka Hook and Ladder Co. No. 1, Minutes, October 4, 1916; Vigilant Engine Co. No. 1, Minutes, October 4, 1916 and November 1, 1916.
14. *Gilroy Advocate*, December 9, 1916.
15. Vigilant Engine Co. No. 1, Minutes, December 7, 1921; Eureka Hook and Ladder Co. No. 1, Minutes, February 10, 1922 and joint agreement dated January 31, 1922.

PALM TREE AND FLAGPOLE: Facade and Accoutrements

1. Interview with George White, May 23, 1986.
2. Gilroy City Council, Minutes, July 6, 1925.
3. Interview, May 23, 1986.

MATRONS, MARSHALS, POLICE AND SHERIFF:
Law Enforcement

1. Interview with George White, May 23, 1986.
2. Followup interview with Virginia Cox, March 25, 1990.
3. Interview, July 7, 1986.
4. Interview, July 7, 1986.
5. Interview with Patricia Baker Loveless, May 23, 1986.

PROPER TOILET AND SANITARY BEDS:
The Jail

1. Gilroy City Council, Minutes, Dec. 4, 1907.
2. Gilroy City Council, Minutes, May 3, 1909.
3. Gilroy City Council, Minutes, Dec. 2, 1912.
4. Gilroy City Council, Minutes, Feb. 4, 1918.
5. Interview, May 23, 1986.
6. Interview, July 7, 1986.
7. Interview with Al Gagliardi, May 23, 1986.

LIKE THE WILD WEST: Gilroy's Justice Court

1. Judge Mark Thomas Jr., "Justices of Pleasant Valley", *In Brief: Official Bulletin of the Santa Clara County Bar Association*, 18 (Spring, 1981), p. 14.
2. Gilroy City Council, Minutes, January 5, 1914.

3. Thomas, "Justices of Pleasant Valley," 16.
4. *Ibid.*
5. *Ibid.*
6. Interview, July 7, 1986.
7. Interview with Al Gagliardi, May 23, 1986.
8. Interview, May 23, 1986.
9. *Ibid.*
10. Interviews, John Klarich and Patricia Baker Loveless, May 23, 1986; County of Santa Clara, *Seismic Safety Plan*, 1975, p. 28.
11. Thomas, "Justices of Pleasant Valley," p. 18.
12. *Gilroy Dispatch*, January 19, 1973 and October 5, 1973.

HEADQUARTERS FOR CIVIL DEFENSE:
World War II

1. Letter from Mary Prien, William Frassetti's sister, July 10, 1986.
2. *Gilroy Advocate*, February 26, 1942.
3. *Gilroy Advocate*, Thursday, October 25, 1942.

THE HUB OF AFFAIRS: City Administration

1. *Gilroy Advocate*, Thursday, January 29, 1942.
2. Interview, July 7, 1986.
3. Gilroy City Council, Minutes, May 7, 1923, and *Gilroy Advocate*, June 23, 1923.
4. Interview, Kendall Pine, March 23, 1990.

OBVIOUS OBSOLESCENCE: The City Hall Under Threat

1. *San Jose Mercury*, April 27, 1958.
2. Gilroy City Council, Minutes, February 15, 1965.
3. Gilroy City Council, Minutes, December 6, 1965.
4. *Gilroy Dispatch*, December 10, 1965.

GRAVE POSSIBILITIES: To Save or to Destroy?

1. Gilroy City Council, Minutes, January 17, 1966.
2. Gilroy City Council, Minutes, February 7, 1966.
3. *Gilroy Dispatch*, February 8, 1966.
4. *Gilroy Dispatch*, March 8, 1966.
5. Letter from Carl Bolfing (circa 1890, as he signed himself) to the Mayor and Councilmen, March 7, 1966; from Records, City of Gilroy.
6. Gilroy City Council, Minutes, March 7, 1966.
7. Gilroy City Council, Minutes, March 21, 1966.
8. *Gilroy Dispatch*, April 5, 1966; Gilroy City Council, Minutes, April 4, 1966.
9. Gilroy City Council, Minutes, April 4, 1966.

BOLFING AT THE HELM: The Gilroy Historical Society is Formed

1. *Gilroy Dispatch*, April 4, 1966.
2. Interview, May 23, 1986.
3. Gilroy City Council, Minutes, July 18, 1966.
4. *Gilroy Dispatch*, July 26, 1966.
5. Interview, May 23, 1986.
6. *Gilroy Dispatch*, July 29, 1966, p.5.
7. Gilroy City Council, Minutes, August 1, 1966.
8. *Gilroy Dispatch*, August 5, 1966.

PROUD AND CONSCIENTIOUS KEEPERS OF THE BUILDING

1. Gilroy City Council, Minutes, October 24, 1966.
2. Interview, May 23, 1986.
3. Interview, May 23, 1986.
4. *Gilroy Dispatch*, March 21, 1967.
5. "Gilroy Residents Save Historic City Hall", *California Historian*, 14 (December, 1967), cover and pp. 45 & 63.
6. Interview with Al Gagliardi, May 23, 1986.
7. Gilroy City Council, Minutes, April 3, 1967.
8. Gilroy City Council, Minutes, January 6, 1969.
9. Gilroy City Council, Minutes, October 2, 1967. The purchase amount was $50.00; the Gilroy Historical Museum now has the sketch.
10. *Gilroy Dispatch*, November 1, 1967.
11. *Gilroy Dispatch*, April 29, 1968.
12. *Gilroy Dispatch*, December 16, 1968, and June 20, 1977.

THE RAREST OF THINGS:
The Museum Within
1. Interview with George White, May 23, 1986.
2. *California Historian*, 14 (December, 1967), p. 63.
3. "Old City Hall stands deserted," *Gilroy Dispatch*, September 8, 1972.
4. *Gilroy Dispatch*, September 11, 1972.
5. *Gilroy Dispatch*, April 29, 1974.

A NATIONAL HISTORIC PLACE: Renovation, Funding and Leasing

1. National Register of Historic Places Inventory, Nomination Form, files, Planning Dept., City of Gilroy.
2. *Gilroy Dispatch*, Dec. 12, 1975.
3. *Gilroy Dispatch*, March 9, 1975.
4. Gilroy Parks and Recreation Department, Memorandum, June 2, 1975.
5. *Gilroy Dispatch*, March 9, 1976.
6. *Gilroy Dispatch*, June 14, 1976.
7. *Gilroy Dispatch*, June 23, 1976.
8. *Gilroy Dispatch*, June 9, 1976.
9. Letter from Gilroy Parks and Recreation Dept., July 21, 1976.
10. *Gilroy Dispatch*, January 7, 1977.
11. *Gilroy Dispatch*, November 19, 1976.
12. *Gilroy Dispatch*, May 6, 1977.
13. *Gilroy Dispatch*, May 27, 1977.
14. *Gilroy Dispatch*, July 20, 1977.
15. Report of the Gilroy Historical Society, July 11, 1977.
16. Interviews with Fred Wood, March 25, 1990, and Jim Farwell, June 6, 1990.
17. *Gilroy Dispatch*, November 20 and 22, 1978.
18. *Gilroy Dispatch*, February 14, 1979.
19. *Gilroy Dispatch*, February 23, 1979.
20. Gilroy City Council, Resolution No. 79-42, May 21, 1979.
21. *Gilroy Dispatch*, June 4 and 6, 1979.
22. *Gilroy Dispatch*, October 24, 1979.
23. *Gilroy Dispatch*, October 31, 1979.

MONTEREY STREET MELT: The Old City Hall Restaurant

1. "Council approves Old City Hall lease," Gilroy Dispatch, Jan.23, 1980.
2. "$10,000 put aside," *Gilroy Dispatch*, January 23, 1980.
3. *Gilroy Dispatch*, December 12, 1980.
4. *Gilroy Dispatch*, July 27, 1981.
5. *Gilroy Dispatch*, September 17, 1982.
6. Interview, Jeff Hoffman, July 1986.
7. *Gilroy Dispatch*, September 21, 1982.
8. *Gilroy Dispatch*, January 24, 1983.
9. *Gilroy Dispatch*, September 22, 1983.
10. *Gilroy Dispatch*, December 27, 1983.
11. Interview with Roberta Hughan, July 7, 1986.

12. Interview with Al Gagliardi, May 23, 1986.
13. *Gilroy Dispatch*, December 27, 1983.
14. Chuck Myer, *Gilroy Dispatch*, June 22, 1984.
15. *Gilroy Dispatch*, April 23, 1985.
16. *Gilroy Dispatch*, June 21, 1985.
17. *Gilroy Dispatch*, July 22, 1985.

II: "THE OLD LADY IS FINE": A New Lease on Life

FROSTING ON THE CAKE: The Old City Hall

1. *Gilroy Dispatch*, April 25, 1985.
2. *Gilroy Dispatch*, August 29, 1985; Old City Hall Committee, Minutes, April 12 and August 10, 1984 and January 3, 1986.
3. *Gilroy Dispatch*, May 14, 1986.
4. Grant Application, Office of Historic Preservation, 1987.
5. Gilroy Dispatch, March 26, 1987.

THE FRED AND ED SPECIAL: The Restaurant Changes Flavors

1. Chuck Myer, *Gilroy Dispatch*, June 22, 1989.
2. *San Jose Mercury-News*, September 26, 1989.

THE QUAKE OF 1989: History Repeats Itself

1. *Gilroy Dispatch*, November 27, 1989.
2. *San Jose Mercury-News*, July 2, 1989.

III. NOT ANOTHER ONE LIKE IT ANYWHERE: The City Hall's Significance

1. *Gilroy Dispatch*, May 20, 1966.
2. Interview, May 23, 1986.
3. Interview, May 23, 1986.
4. Interview, May 23, 1986.
5. Interview, July 7, 1986.

APPENDIX A: Mayors and Council Members Who Served In The Old City Hall

AUTHORIZING COUNCIL 1904:
"PROGRESSIVE PARTY"
Mayor: George T. Dunlap
Council: Valentine Grodhaus
George Milias Sr.
James Princevalle
Marshal Rice
George Seay
Robert E. Wood

1906
Mayor: George T. Dunlap
Council: Luke Feeny
Harry Frutig
Charles N. Hoover
George Milias Sr.
James Princevalle
James White

1908
Mayor: Walter G. Fitzgerald
Council: A. A. Martin
P. W. Parmelee
Daniel J. Riley
William B. Stuart
Dr. James W. Thayer
Robert E. Wood

1910
Mayor: A. A. Martin
Council: Henry L. McDuffee
P. W. Parmelee
Daniel J. Riley
William B. Stuart
Henry L. Wilds
Robert E. Wood

1912

Mayor: A. A. Martin

Council: George A. Chappell

             Maxwell J. Crow

             Lawrence S. Cullen

             James McElroy

             P. W. Parmelee

             Daniel J. Riley

1914

Mayor: George A. Wentz

Council: Arthur W. Chesbro

             Dr. John A. Clark

             Charles E. Fredrickson

             James Princevalle

             George S. Tremaine

             Henry L. Wilds

1916

Mayor: George A. Wentz

Council: Arthur W. Chesbro

             Dr. John A. Clark

             Charles E. Fredrickson

             James Princevalle

             George S. Tremaine

             Henry L. Wilds

1918

Mayor: Herbert E. Robinson

Council: Maxwell J. Crow

             Charles Fredrickson

             Robert M. Martin

             James Princevalle

             Charles Schemel

             Rowley M. Thomas

1920

Mayor: James Princevalle

Council: Arthur W. Brown

             Elmer J. Chesbro, M.D.

             Charles C. Lester

             Robert M. Martin

             William Radtke

             Charles Schemel

1922

Mayor: James Princevalle

Council: Arthur W. Brown

             Elmer J. Chesbro, M.D.

             Gerald Hecker

             Charles C. Lester

             William Radtke

             Charles W. Schemel

1924

Mayor: James Princevalle

Council: Richard Brem

             Charles Fredrickson

             Gerald Hecker

             Charles Pierce

             William Radtke

             Charles W. Schemel

1926

Mayor: James Princevalle

Council: Jerome Chappell

             Elmer J. Chesbro, M.D.

             Charles Fredrickson

             Gerald Hecker

             E. Martin Johnson

             Charles H. Pierce

1928

Mayor: James Princevalle

Council: Elmer J. Chesbro, M.D.

             Dr. John A. Clark

             Walter G. Fitzgerald

             Charles E. Fredrickson

             Irvin Hollister

             E. Martin Johnson

1930

Mayor: James Princevalle
Council: Fred. C. Boock
          George Easton
          Charles Fredrickson
          Stephen D. Heck
          George Lawton
          J. Hardin Rush

1932

Mayor: Elmer J. Chesbro, M.D.
Council: Fred. C. Boock
          George Easton
          Stephen D. Heck
          George C. Milias
          J. Hardin Rush
          George A. Wentz

1934

Mayor: Elmer J. Chesbro, M.D.
Council: Fred. C. Boock
          Stephen D. Heck
          George C. Milias
          J. Hardin Rush
          W. Benjamin Stewart
          George A. Wentz

1936

Mayor: Stephen D. Heck
Council: Nathaniel Heiner
          George Mason
          George C. Milias
          J. Hardin Rush
          W. Benjamin Stewart
          Henry Wilkinson

1938

Mayor: Stephen D. Heck
Council: James K. Battersby
          Nathaniel Heiner
          George Martin
          George Mason
          George C. Milias
          Jack Rogers

1940

Mayor: George C. Milias
Council: James K. Battersby
          Nathaniel Heiner
          George Martin
          George Mason
          Jack Rogers
          John Wentworth

1942

Mayor: George C. Milias
Council: James K. Battersby
          Nathaniel Heiner
          George Martin
          George Mason
          David Stout
          John Wentworth

1944

Mayor: George C. Milias
Council: Nathaniel Heiner
          George Martin
          George Mason
          Henry Schilling
          David Stout
          John Wentworth

1946

Mayor: George C. Milias
Council: Nathaniel Heiner
          George Martin
          George Mason
          Raymond Stevens
          J. Benjamin Thomas
          John Wentworth

1948

Mayor: George C. Milias
Council: David Daniels
George Mason
Raymond Stevens
David Stout
J. Benjamin Thomas
John Wentworth

1950

Mayor: George C. Milias
Council: David Daniels
George Mason
Carl W. Pate
David Stout
J. Benjamin Thomas
John Wentworth

1952

Mayor: George C. Milias
Council: Charles Gallo
J. Hughes Kennedy
Carl W. Pate
Jack E. Ronald
Courtland Rush
George White

1954

Mayor: George Mason
Council: Charles Gallo
J. Hughes Kennedy
Carl W. Pate
Kenneth Petersen
Courtland Rush
Sig Sanchez

1956

Mayor: George C. Milias
Council: Charles Gallo
Carl W. Pate
Kenneth Petersen
Courtland Rush
Sig Sanchez
Everett Wentworth

1958

Mayor: Sig Sanchez
Council: Charles Gallo
Wilford E. Jordan
Carl W. Pate
Kenneth Petersen
Courtland Rush
Everett Wentworth

APPENDIX B: City Staff Serving in the Old City Hall

CITY CLERKS

1900-1906	C. Newton Hoover
1906-1937	Eugene F. Rogers d. 1-29-1937 Deputy Clerk, Philip A. Cox, Appointed to remainder of term.
1937-1957	Philip A. Cox d. 6-23-1957 Deputy Clerk, Graydon B. Carr, Appointed to remainder of term.
1957-1960	Graydon B. Carr

New City Charter was enacted on February 8, 1960.

2-15-1960 to Present	Susanne Thomas Steinmetz appointed as City Clerk when Graydon B. Carr was appointed as City Administrator.

CITY TREASURERS

1894-1916	Henry Hecker
1916-1930	Julia Allen Haselbach
1930-1938	Robert Colson
1938-1940	Paul Tremaine
1940-1942	Ethel Tremaine
1942-1960	E. Rodney Eschenberg
1960	Office abolished under the new charter

CITY MARSHALS

1904-1906	A. B. Ward
1906-1916	Henry T. Mayock
1916-1930	George Easton
1930-1938	Walter S. White
1938-1952	A.G. Goodrich
1952-1960	Harold Sturla
1960	Office abolished under new charter; title changed to Chief of Police; C.J. Laizure appointed.

JUSTICES OF THE PEACE

1883-1919	Howard Willey and John Baillaige
1919-1931	John M. Hoesch
1931-1959	Leon T. Thomas
1959-1973	John M. Klarich

APPENDIX C: Original Letter From "Pop" Bolfing

346 North Hanna Street
Gilroy, California
March 7, 1966

Honorable Mayor and Councilmen;

Thank you for considering my thoughts on razing the old City Hall.

To begin with this building represents the civic pride and sacrifices of the people of Gilroy of 1905; a time when the tax dollar was hard to come by, but the urge for personal sacrifice was strong. I believe they deserve our consideration.

The razing of the building and making a sightly corner involves a cost that no one seems able to guarantee. This corner on Monterey Street should not be turned into a public parking lot and is not a proper facility for the City as a whole to undertake. Therefore I propose that we take this cost and add to it the amount that normally should have been spent for repairs and maintenance for the past ten

Opposite:

October 1977. *The Gilroy Museum*

or more years, to put the building back into reasonable condition for a limited use. There would be very little difference to make up. The engineering figures mean little because no one suggests that more than reasonable repairs be made for limited use. To bring the whole structure up to modern standards - standards that few buildings in the City would meet - should not be considered.

Of course a museum is the logical use when restored. This plan should include purchase of the old Winkler property and the landscaping of the surrounding area with a few parking spaces for visitors and tourists that may be interested enough to stop and have a look at the old building, do a little shopping or whatever. The parking should not be used for local shoppers. Sign it so that visitors to our City would know we welcome them.

Every City has a need of something with which to identify. Tombstone has its City Hall - Eureka, its Carson House - Jackson, its Louisiana Hotel - Mariposa and Bridgeport their old courthouses and Carson City its Mint Museum. All of these are known throughout the United States and bring these cities untold advertising that comes in no other way.

Gilroy someday will be right along with them, if

we of today just have the vision. Don't sell the old City Hall short as an advertising asset.

Taking the above steps would encourage the formation of a Gilroy Historical Society to implement the organizing of a museum that will depict "Who, what and why Gilroy is." I would be willing to help organize such a society.

In restoring the old building, the lower floor could be returned to it's original use (which was the fire house) and used for the old fire equipment and relics of the 1905 era. The old jail could be used in the same manner for items of early police use and records, with the upper floor as a general display area. With the eyes and minds of many interested workers we might just be surprised what would be brought to light.

Before steps are taken that cannot be retraced, just give these thoughts consideration. There is not another symbol of early Gilroy left that can give Gilroy identity and there are just a lot of us old Gilroyans that hate to see this last chance be lost.

Come up with a realistic plan and a realistic cost and we will all be with you.

Carl N. Bolfing
circa 1890

SUBJECT INDEX (Including Appendices)

Tremaine, George S., 110

University of California, 60, 88
U.S. government. *See* National Park Service;
    National Register of Historic Places; Post Office,
    U.S.; Small Business Administration

Vicars, Joel, III, 88
Vigilant Engine Company, 33, 34, 37
Vigna, Frances Cullen Howson, xi, 43, 99
Vigna, Frances Howson, 29
Volunteer Fire Department, 4, 6
    consolidated, 37
    Fifth Street Fire House, 27, 36
    new equipment for, 33-36
        Seagrave pumper, 69
    See also Eureka Hook and Ladder Company; Fire
        Department; Vigilant Engine Company

Ward, A. B., 113
Watsonville, 79
Webber, Helen, 88
Weber, C. F. & Company, 20
Wentworth Everett, 112
Wentworth, John, 111, 112
Wentz, George A., 110, 111
Wheeler Auditorium, 55, 57
White, Armand, 63
White, George, xi, 39, 63, 67, 68, 71, 112
Whitehurst, Mr., 12
White, James, 109
White, John A. Jr., 89
White, John E., 39, 41
White, Walter S., 41, 113
Whitmore, Richard K., 51
Wilds, Henry L. 109, 110
Wilkinson, Henry, 111
Willey, Howard, 45, 113
Williams, James C., xi, 85, 88
Williams, J. W., 8

Wilson, Mr., 18
Winkler's harness shop, 1, 6, 11, 115
Wolfe Frank D. , 8
    City Hall plans by, 8, 9-11, 12
    during Hall construction, 12, 16
    earthquake damage inspection by, 17
Wolfe and McKenzie, 4, 6, 18, 20
    City Hall blueprint by, 10
Women's Civic Club, 31
Wood, Fred O., xi, 64, 78
Wood, Robert E., 109
Woollacott, Angela, 88
World War I, in Gilroy, 29
World War II, in Gilroy, 49-51
Wright, Claude, 68